THE OFFICE OF ASSERTION

THE OFFICE OF ASSERTION

An Art of Rhetoric for the Academic Essay

SCOTT F. CRIDER

ISI Books
Wilmington, Delaware
2005

Crider, Scott F.

   The office of assertion : an art of rhetoric for the academic
   essay / Scott F. Crider. — 1st ed. — Wilmington, Del. : ISI
   Books, 2005.

      p. ; cm.

      Includes bibliographical references.
      ISBN: 1932236457

      1. Rhetoric. 2. English language—Rhetoric. 3. Essay—
Authorship. 4. Academic writing. I. Title

P301.5.A27 C75 2005   2004104558
808.4—dc22   0506

Published in the United States by:

   ISI Books
   Post Office Box 4431
   Wilmington, DE 19807-0431

         www.isibooks.org

      Book design by Kara Beer
   Manufactured in the United States of America

Dedicated to David Bell,
Marc Bertonasco, and
John Briggs,
good men skilled in speaking

We are speaking where we stand, and we shall stand afterwards in the presence of what we have said.

Wendell Berry
Standing by Words

Table of Contents

Preface

Having looked unsuccessfully far and wide for a very short rhetoric to use in my literature courses, I decided to write one. I found most rhetorics, even those I still very much admire, overly long, developed, and encyclopedic—that is, better consulted than read all the way through. I wanted a shorter treatment: a long essay, not a textbook. Too many others were written with far too low a view of both students' intellects and rhetoric's nature. You have in your hands, then, a brief but serious rhetoric, one which can be read profitably in a weekend and which, for the interested student, can be used as an introduction to the classical art of rhetoric and composition. The works cited form a select library for the more advanced student to pursue. I think this book could be used as the rhetoric in any humanities course, including first-year composition, supplemented perhaps only with a handbook. Though I do think that advanced high school students, homeschoolers, and even professional writers will find the book profitable, it has been written primarily to the first-year college student.

Four of the book's characteristics require comment. First, it is informed both by the classical rhetorical tradition and more recent discoveries concerning the writing process. Second, because I teach literature in a school with a core curriculum founded on great books, the approach is admittedly old-fashioned and assumes that the reader is interested in writing about those texts which have proven to be essential for anyone who wishes to understand, rather than simply dwell within, the contemporary world. One of the reasons I have used a student essay on Homer is my belief that students write better when they write about difficult and important texts, especially those central to so many other texts. I hope the Homeric material will not be distracting for a general reader who may not yet have read Homer. Indeed, my desire is that such a reader will be inspired to read Homer's foundational poems. The end here is in no way reactionary. What both celebrants and critics of multicultural education have failed to understand is this: culture has always already been multicultural. There is no avoiding either the past or the present, because the important texts of our own present culture are themselves intertextual responses to past ones. One of the contemporary world's most important poems, Derek Walcott's *Omeros*, for example, is a poem which at once relies upon and redefines its Homeric intertexts. I shall ignore the culture war over curriculum because I believe it to be one long either-or fallacy. Third, the book discusses only one kind of writing: the academic essay. This is certainly not the only form of the genre, and I applaud the attempt to enlarge the kinds of writing we ask students to produce. I have assigned dramatic scenes, poems, and journals myself. Even so, most classes require an academic essay. My vision of what rhetoric is would certainly encompass many other forms of writing, perhaps even all, but the focus here is quite limited and highly practical. Last, the book assumes and argues that the writing that students do for teachers *matters,* that in itself such writing is perhaps one of the most important intellectual, emotional, and spiritual experiences in the life that students and teachers share. Whatever the soul may be exactly, it must be acknowledged by anyone, teacher or student, who hopes to be a good rhetor.

Acknowledgments

I would like to thank the University of Dallas, especially its Department of English, for encouraging me in this project and providing release time to complete it.

John Alvis, Ray DiLorenzo, Eileen Gregory, Greg Roper, Kathryn Smith, Glen Thurow, Gerard Wegemer, and Kas Zoller have been invaluable friends of the enterprise. Jeremy Beer, David Bell, John Briggs, Bill Frank, and Lance Simmons each gave the book an exacting, helpful reading. Wayne Ambler, then Dean of the UD Rome Program, encouraged me to use this book as the basis for the writing program in Rome while I was there, an experience which encouraged me greatly. I would also like to thank the tutors in the UD Writing Lab for assistance and advice from 1994 to 2004, especially the Directors of the Writing Program during that period: Joel Garza, Lisa Marciano, and Andrew Moran.

Since 1994, I have been fortunate to know a large number of fine students, from whose essays I have learned a great deal about the teaching of writing.

Many have commented upon parts of the book, and their readings have proven most helpful. I would like to thank all of them, especially Tommy Heyne, whose essay I use here to exemplify fine undergraduate writing, and Ruth Fiegenshue, whose essay I used in an earlier manuscript. I might have included a great many more essays from my students of the last ten years. An early student, Lynn Schofield, is now a teacher herself, and her use of—and comments upon—the manuscript were especially astute and encouraging.

I would like to thank Sharen Craft-Baker, Karen Boyd, and Karen Gempel for their invaluable administrative assistance.

Special thanks go to Diane Crider, whose loving and continual correction of my speech when I was a boy remains an inspiration.

Final thanks are owed Trang Crider, whose intelligent and kind grace is itself an argument, and our son Kiên, already a talented rhetor.

This small book is dedicated to three mentors, each in his distinct way a Quintilian. I am able to write it only because all of them had the courage and patience to read student essays with care and to assume, on sometimes rather scant evidence, that they could be improved. I wish the book were as good as their standards demanded.

Chapter–Paragraph Outline

Below is an outline of the book by chapter and paragraph. Within the text, I will often cross-reference discussions by including in bold brackets the chapter and paragraph of the matter discussed, e.g., *[1.2]*.

1. Introduction: Rhetoric as the Liberal Art of Soul-Leading in Writing

2. Invention:
The Discovery of Arguments

3. Organization:
The Desire for Design

4. Style:
Words and Sentences

1

Introduction: Rhetoric as the Liberal Art of Soul-Leading in Writing

[1.1] "Rhetoric" is a term of abuse, of course: Immediately after someone has distorted the truth during an interview on television, for example, the journalist will comment, "We know that was just rhetoric." Rhetoric: this pejorative term now means any language, spoken or written, which is misleading or actually untrue. There is reality, and there is rhetoric. As a consequence of such usage, my readers may be surprised to learn that they will be studying this suspect art in order to learn how to write the academic essay. In fact, the art of rhetoric has always been suspect in the Western philosophical tradition, an outlaw of disciplines only occasionally allowed respectability; even so, many of the most important figures in the Western intellectual tradition were indeed trained in this art. In literature, the epic poets Virgil, Ovid, Dante, and Milton were themselves educated in rhetoric, and Homer arguably invented it. Shakespeare's schooling was thoroughly rhetorical. In philosophy, rhetoric's most thoughtful critics, Plato and Augustine, were both trained in rhetoric, and Augustine was himself a teacher of the art, even after his conversion to Christianity. Nietzsche was a professor of rhetoric. Even the "anti-philosopher" Jacques Derrida hoped to revive the art of rhetoric, though in its sophistic form. In politics, the founders of the American regime were rhetoricians, in part because they were lawyers, but more importantly because they were liberally educated, and, until very recently, a liberal education in the humanities was a rhetorical education. Jefferson, Madison, Lincoln, Cady-Stanton, King: these American leaders were all students of the art of rhetoric. Arousing both fear and interest, rhetoric has always been suspect, but it has still, interestingly, always been studied.

[1.2] The fear is mistaken, but the interest is not. This small book has two rather large rhetorical purposes of its own. On the one hand, it has a highly practical goal: improving the reader's writing, especially of the academic essay. It will examine rhetoric as a productive art, the principled process of *making* a product, in this case an essay. On the other hand, it also has a more general goal: persuading the reader that rhetoric, as both a productive and a liberal art, is a good thing. To argue that rhetoric is a liberal art is hardly common. Intellectuals in both the humanities and the sciences generally believe that rhetoric is a corrupt form of inquiry—those in the humanities convinced either that its calculation precludes sincerity or that its informal reasoning precludes seriousness, those in the sciences convinced that its interest in the emotions precludes objectivity. As well, some in the humanities actually concede that rhetoric is not interested in truth, yet then defend it on those grounds; for them, rhetoric is composed of the rules of any discourse, and an interest in the truth or falsity of any word is naïve. Though they may or may not realize it, they are defending, not rhetoric, but sophistry. (We will return to this in a moment.) I grant that rhetoric is often misused, and I grant that it has its own limitations as an art. Many good things are limited, though, and there is nothing that cannot be abused. The misuse of rhetoric, according to Aristotle in the *Rhetoric*, does not condemn it:

> If it is argued that one who makes an unfair use of such a faculty of speech may do a great deal of harm, this objection applies equally to all good things except virtue, and above all to those things which are most useful, such as health, wealth, generalship; for as these, rightly used, may be of the greatest benefit, so, wrongly used, they may do an equal amount of harm. (1.1.13)

Rhetoric is no more essentially destructive than physics. There is no need to fear this art. As the reader's writing improves, he or she should experience an increasing intellectual power. This power is a good power, even if the student were to misuse it. When a journalist exposes misleading or untrue statements, for example, that is a good thing. What the journalist simply may not recognize, or will not admit to the audience, is that the exposure is just as rhetorical as the statement exposed. The art of rhetoric is not unjust; those who use it unjustly are. As Aristotle explains, "What makes one a sophist is not the faculty but the moral purpose" (1.1.14). Aristotle believes that rhetoric and sophistry are distinct: rhetoric is persuasion aimed at the truth; sophistry is persuasion aimed only at the appearance of truth. This book, then, offers a defense of rhetoric. The most important of its proofs is that rhetoric is a liberal art which liberates one both to defend oneself against untrue persuasions and to fashion true ones. Often, those untrue persuasions are one's own; after all, we are all familiar with the sophist within, that part of us who arises, especially in haste or anger, to utter sham arguments, arguments that—in calmer, more reflective moments—we know are mistaken. So rhetoric can free one even from one's own ignorance, disclosing the weaknesses of one's own idea; having done so, it can then free others. Indeed, in freeing others, one frees oneself. I realize that this is quite a claim. After defining rhetoric and examining its constituent appeals and parts, I will make good on it.

[1.3] According to Aristotle, rhetoric is "the faculty of discovering the possible means of persuasion in reference to any subject whatever" (**1.2.1**). We need to discuss that definition at length. There are three essential parts to the definition. Generally, rhetoric is a faculty of mind. Two other aspects differentiate it from other such faculties: first, this faculty of mind discovers means of persuasion; second, it does so in particular circumstances. Rhetoric is not a formula, but a faculty; though it involves formulae, it is not essentially formulaic. A formula is a "rule" of composition, but such "rules" are themselves the result of thought. For example, every reader of this book is likely a master of a contemporary formula of composition, the Five-Paragraph Essay. The "rule" is this: every essay has five paragraphs—an introduction, three points, and a conclusion. Three other formulae follow: The introduction should begin generally and funnel into one's thesis, the last sentence of the first paragraph; the next three paragraphs should be numbered—first, second, and third; and, finally, the conclusion should summarize the essay and funnel out toward some very general point. One can write such an essay without much reflection at all. Here is a very brief Five-Paragraph Essay:

> Eating is important. Because everyone eats, restaurants have an important social purpose. My favorite restaurant is McDonald's. I like McDonald's for three reasons.

First, I like McDonald's because the food is very good. The Big Mac is particularly tasty, so I order one every time I go there.

Second, I like McDonald's because the food is inexpensive. I can eat lunch for under four dollars. This means that I can eat there often.

Third, I like McDonald's because someone I don't like works there, and, while I enjoy my inexpensive lunch, I can watch him slave over the grill for minimum wage.

In conclusion, I like McDonald's because the food is good and inexpensive, and the staff entertaining.

Does this essay sound familiar? The reader's essays have been much more subtle, no doubt; even so, once a formula is so easy to parody, it has probably lost its persuasive force. This formula does do limited work, granted, and there may be rhetorical situations when it is appropriate, even graceful. But the formula is not very flexible. Some of the "rules" of composition are often not rules at all, then. There are rhetorical principles which usually operate in most situations; there are even formulae which make composition much easier. In fact, the Five-Paragraph Essay is a variation of a much more flexible, classical shape that we will examine in Chapter 3. But rhetoric is not essentially those formulae; essentially, it is the faculty of discovering them. The Greek for "faculty" is *dunamis*, "power or capacity"; *dunamis* is the root of the English word "dynamism." Rhetoric is the power or capacity of the mind to discover, the actualization of a human intellectual potential that, when actualized, releases energy.

[1.4] So far, of course, that is true of any other discipline. The first *differentia*, or distinguishing characteristic, separating rhetoric from other disciplines is that it is always discovering means of persuasion. For Aristotle, philosophy discovers truth; rhetoric, the means of convincing an audience of that truth. However, rhetoric often helps us discover what we believe about a subject as well, even as we are learning how to convince an audience of its truth. Although Aristotle probably would not agree, philosophy does not always precede rhetoric; instead, rhetoric is often an occasion for philosophy. As one searches for means of persuasion about one's subject, one learns more about it. Generally, there are three "means of persuasion": *logos, pathos,* and *ethos*—the logical, emotional, and ethical appeals. All three are legitimate, and all three are part of any suasion. *Logos,* though, is the primary appeal in academic rhetoric. One argues that one's case is the most reasonable. At times, one will arouse and direct a reader's emotion; at times, one will represent oneself in such a way as to establish one's own intellectual and moral authority. Even so, *logos*—to repeat— is the central appeal in academic discourse. Rhetoric, then, is here the faculty of discovering the most convincing *logos.*

[1.5]   Rhetoric's second *differentia* is contingency. The rhetorical faculty of discovering the most convincing *logos* always operates in particular circumstances. One does not always argue in the same way regardless of circumstance. Although there are general principles of persuasion, one must accommodate variables, four of which we need to examine here: genre, subject, audience, and purpose. First, different genres—or kinds of writing—lead to different resources. For example, if one is writing a letter, one would probably be better served imitating another letter rather than a short story. (I will not discuss this generic variable since the present book concerns only the academic essay.) Second, different subjects entail different appeals: each discipline looks at the world differently, a disciplinary vision always both allowing some arguments and precluding others. The papers you wrote in high school for English probably differed from those you wrote for history. The general method of rhetorical investigation is always in creative tension with disciplinary methods. An academic subject demands certain appeals; particular subjects then demand even more refined ones. Third, different audiences demand different approaches. One does not write a letter or an e-mail message the same way to a sibling as to a parent, for example. Academic audiences, in particular, are peculiar. Educated, critical—even impatient—the academic is a difficult audience to write for. Academics expect that students will be like them, and one of the things you learn at a university is the "way" to respond academically to the world. You imitate your professors to learn that "way," not necessarily by parroting their actual arguments—though a few demand just that—but instead by imitating their methods of argumentation. Indeed, one of the purposes of academic rhetoric is to learn that "way." Fourth, different purposes demand different appeals. The reader may believe that the primary purpose of academic writing is a good grade; such a grade is only a sign, however, a sign of achievement. Your primary rhetorical purpose in academic writing should be to achieve and share the intellectual excellence or virtue of understanding. Regardless of the subject, regardless of the professor, the best student is the one whose written work persuades the reader—whether a faculty member, a tutor, or a fellow student—to take pleasure in the operation of such a mind. That pleasure is educational, the pleasure of experiencing a free mind releasing the energy of *logos*. Using Aristotle's definition of rhetoric, one can see its substance: writing within a genre to an audience about a subject, the rhetor finds means of persuasion to achieve the end of persuasion, whose own yet further end is understanding.

[1.6] We can now see that rhetoric is the intellectual power to discover, even fashion, formulae to persuade an academic audience to believe that one's argument about the subject at hand is true. Having defined rhetoric, we are ready to examine its three parts, discrete but related elements of the art of com-position: invention, organization, and style. This examination will be brief because each is the focus of its own chapter. In short, invention is what you argue; organization, in what order you argue; style, how you argue. (In the classical rhetorical tradition, there were two other elements, memory and deliv-ery, both of which are essential to spoken rhetoric, but not to written.) An essay's substance is the in-vention or discovery both of the argument that guides the proofs, or points, and of the proofs that themselves defend that argument. Though inven-tion is necessary, it is not, however, sufficient; that is, it has to be present, but other things have to be present as well. The discovered matter has to be shaped, given form. Organization gives form to the argumentative matter, providing a beginning, a middle, and an end to the small universe of the es-say. The ordered substance must then be communi-cated through the medium of style, the words and sentences that carry the reader through that small universe.

[1.7]   The parts of rhetoric provide the shape of this book. I will explain invention in much greater detail in Chapter 2; organization, in Chapter 3; and style, in Chapter 4. In Chapter 5, I will explain how these three parts can operate as a writing process: A first draft invents; a second arranges; a third styl-izes. This three-part understanding of the essay informs my discussion of one student's essay on Homer's *Odyssey*, an essay I have included to indicate not only that undergraduates can write excellent essays, but also that they can master difficult and important texts.

[1.8] How does the art of rhetoric defined and outlined above liberate both rhetorician and audience, though? By providing the writer with the power to give shape to the reader's world. Richard Weaver, in *The Ethics of Rhetoric*, offers a fine explanation of just this phenomenon:

> [T]he right to utter a sentence is one of the very greatest liberties; and we are entitled to little wonder that freedom of utterance should be, in every society, one of the most contentious and ill-defined rights. The liberty to impose this formal unity is a liberty to handle the world, to remake it, if only a little, and to hand it to others in a shape which may influence their actions. It is interesting to speculate whether the Greeks did not, for this very reason, describe the man clever at speech as *deinos*, an epithet meaning, in addition to "clever," "fearful" and "terrible." The sentence through its *office of assertion* is a force adding itself to the forces of the world, and therefore the man clever with his sentences . . . was regarded with that uneasiness we feel in the presence of power. The changes wrought by

sentences are changes in the world rather than
the physical earth, but it is to be remembered
that changes in the world bring about changes
in the earth. (118-19, my emphasis)

The study of rhetoric educates one in a particular
liberty, the "liberty to handle the world, to remake
it, if only a little, and to hand it to others in a shape
which may influence their actions." Through this
"office of assertion," the writer is a leader of souls.
As Plato explains in the *Phaedrus*, rhetoric is "the art
of soul-leading by means of words" (261a). Each time
one asks another person to read one's work, one is
in the Socratic position of leading that reader
through the small world of the essay, a reading experience that gives shape somehow to the world itself. Ray DiLorenzo argues in *Peitho: A Classical Rhetoric* that rhetoric is "the care of words and things";
that care is associative, a practice one learns—and
never stops learning—in the presence of others, the
ones you lead and are led by. Such soul-leading is a
liberal power, one which in its finest and fullest
manifestation is a form of love: the finest rhetorician not only loves wisdom, but also loves others
who do so. The finest rhetor, then, is a friend. As
Aristotle explains in the *Nicomachean Ethics*, "The
perfect form of friendship is that between the good,
and those who resemble each other in virtue" (8.3.6).
The best university is a rhetorical community of
friends, and the ultimate purpose of this book is to
teach the reader how to live within such a commu-

nity with words so full of care that they release the light of brilliance.

[1.9] It is, of course, the nature of a liberal art that its study is a good in and of itself, regardless of its utility as a means to some other end. As John Henry Newman puts it in *The Idea of a University*, knowledge, "prior to its being a power . . . is a good; it is not only an instrument, but an end" (137). Rhetoric is certainly a powerful instrument, but, I will argue, it is also an object of knowledge that is good in and of itself. It is difficult to imagine that rhetoric *could* be such an art; after all, its end is persuasion, and persuasion by its very nature involves yet a further end. The rhetor persuades his or her audience to believe and/or to do something else. This is often the case, granted. Even so, in its highest form, rhetoric reflects upon such further ends, even if from within its own highly contingent circumstances. What is the end of persuasion in an academic community? The truth of the matter at hand, not as an object possessed, but as a disposition toward the subject, a disposition that is truer than before the rhetorical moment, a disposition shared with one's audience. That disposition is, according to Socrates, the highest good of human life, for, as he would have it, the unexamined life is not worth living. The care of words and things—that is, the care of things through the care of words—in a generous, disciplined forum: this human activity is rhetorical throughout, the true influence of friends who have, as Phaedrus puts it at the close of the *Phaedrus*, "everything in common" (279c), in particular the shared motion toward the real. As you can see, we will be discussing more than punctuation.

2

Invention:

The Discovery of Arguments

[2.1] The professor sits down to read, comment upon, and grade a set of papers on the *Odyssey*. The first essay begins: "I don't like Odysseus. He is so sneaky. I don't really care what happens to him." The professor, pausing to teach, writes in the margin a comment: "Where is your argument?" Reading on, he or she discovers that there is none and fails the essay. In fact, most beginning writers fail to invent an argument, in the proper sense of the phrase: either they repeat some idea or interpretation that they know their reader approves of, or they express an opinion, even a mere impression, that they believe should persuade the reader simply because it is the writer's. Opinions, though, have varying degrees of persuasive force, and a student's opinion must be believed by the reader only if the writer makes that opinion persuasive. And its persuasiveness will depend on four general characteristics: The opinion must be focused; it must be articulated as a

15

proposition; and it must be supported by both a development of its ideas and an explication of the idea, event, text, or artifact involved, explication that both analyzes a part of the object and synthesizes the parts of it into a comprehension of the whole object. I will concentrate on arguments about texts because they are still the most common in courses in the humanities and because they can exemplify arguments about ideas, events, and artifacts.

[2.2]   The rhetorician's first goal is to sharpen the focus of the rhetorical enterprise. First, one should read the essay prompt very carefully. Most prompts are either questions that must be answered or positions that must be argued for or against.

The problem with even the best prompts is that they might prompt essays much longer than the one the student is actually going to write. If one's limit is 500 to 750 words, most prompts will require that the writer provide a very sharp focus. Your essay is like a map of a territory: the smaller the map, the smaller the territory that can be adequately represented by it. A map of the earth is not a map of America; a map of America is not a map of your state; a map of your state is not a map of your city; a map of your city is not a map of your university. If one wanted to find a classroom on your campus, a map of your state would be useless because it would lack the focus needed. As with maps, so with essays. The writer must ascertain what is possible with respect to the circumstances, in this case the circumstance of scale. A two- or three-page essay requires a very tight focus. If, for example, one is fashioning an argument about Odysseus's mental versatility, trying to decide if he is prudent or merely cunning, one might not be able to discuss all the episodes in which he exhibits that versatility, nor to examine all the differences between prudence and cunning; instead, one would probably want to isolate one episode or one difference, perhaps the episode in which he deceives Penelope, and the end for which he deceives her. Sharpening the focus allows one to prosecute rather than assume the case. Calling him "sneaky" and presuming that a reader will then agree is hardly compelling.

[2.3] Once focused, an essay must have an argument to govern it: a thesis. What is a thesis? A thesis is a proposition determinate enough to provide unity and coherence to the essay: it declares something about the subject at hand, what it declares is limited in scope, and that limitation ensures that the essay will be about one thing that will hold together the essay's constituent parts. According to Edward Corbett in *Classical Rhetoric for the Modern Student*, "The cardinal principle is to state the thesis in a single declarative sentence" (47). A declarative sentence is a sentence that can be affirmed or denied; that is, it is arguable, a sentence about which intelligent and principled people can disagree. There must be an argumentative subject, often the grammatical subject of the sentence, and there must be a predication about the subject *[4.7]*. Though a thesis may begin, during the writing process, as an impression, it is not an impression. Though a thesis may necessitate an outline of its proofs *[3.7]*, such an outline is not a thesis. A thesis is the distillation of the essay, the one identifiable point that a reader must believe if the writer demonstrates its truth. Here, for example, is an impression masquerading as a thesis: "I don't like Odysseus." Who can disagree? Here is an adequate thesis with the potential to be a fine one: "Odysseus is not prudent, but cunning." It certainly declares something; it is arguable. There is an argumentative subject—Odysseus—and there is a predication which declares that he is cunning. The problem is that the declaration is not determinate enough to ensure unity and coherence. In rhetoric, fortunately, problems become resources; when one recognizes a weakness in one's written work, one may improve it through revision *[5]*. Revised, the above thesis might become quite a bit stronger: "Odysseus is cunning, not prudent, because, long after he can be sure of Penelope's fidelity, he continues to try to deceive her." Notice that what provides determination is the reason for the first impression. A thesis will not include all one's proofs, but it must provide the essence of the case, the distilled point the proofs will defend.

[2.4]   The thesis will require demonstration, proofs that argue for the truth of the proposition. Such demonstration takes two forms: The proposition and its terms must be clarified and developed; and the clear, developed proposition must make sense of the object of analysis—the text. What does it mean to develop an argument? We tend to assume that our argument is self-evident, either because we ourselves already understand it and simply expect others to, or because we have not thought enough about it to see that its terms might need to be defined and its ideas elaborated. If one argues that Odysseus is not prudent, but only cunning, though, then one must have some definition, if only assumed, of prudence. Hence, an argument about Odysseus's prudence will have to define the nature of prudence, establish some standard of the virtue he either is or is not meeting, and distinguish prudence from cunning. There are two ways to develop an idea: one can draw on either the syllogisms of logic or the topics of invention. These methods of development are not exclusive, but it helps to examine each individually. Let's first examine logic, analyzing Jefferson's "Declaration of Independence," then examine the topics, analyzing Madison's *Federalist* 10. Our country was founded, after all, by people who comprehended rhetorical invention.

[2.5]   Logic is founded on a principle, often called a "law": the principle of non-contradiction (PNC).

In the *Metaphysics*, Aristotle provides a characteristically lucid description of the PNC: "It is impossible for anything at the same time to be and not be" (1006a3–4). Were one to testify in a court of law that one was at home at a particular time and another witness were to testify that he or she saw you somewhere else at that same time, a judge and jury would have to conclude, by logical necessity, that one of the witnesses was mistaken or deceptive. The PNC explains why; it operates as a foundation upon which reason rests. Hence, if you argue in your introduction to an essay on Shakespeare's *Hamlet* that Hamlet believes that revenge is right, but—during the writing process *[5]*—change your mind and conclude that he does not, then fail to revise for consistency, your reader will be confused: "Does he, or doesn't he?" Arguments that contradict themselves are not very persuasive. The PNC cannot be proven, by the way; it is simply assumed in all rational discourse. This point helps to explain why essays that fail to obey this elementary law of reason impress a reader as "crazy." Yet inconsistencies in our thought often dwell so deep within the argument that we cannot, without assistance, even recognize that there is, in fact, an inconsistency. If you argue A on your first page and -A (i.e., the reverse of A) on your last, then you will probably see the inconsistency if you re-read your own work before turning it in. However, if you argue A throughout your essay but in one proof assume X to defend it and in another -X, you may not recognize it until your professor points it out in his or her comments. Even then, you may not see it immediately.

[2.6]   Why? Because assumptive arguments are not easily observable. Deduction is more difficult than induction. Induction—often called loosely "the scientific method"—consists of observing particularities that establish a principle. One of the features of Darwin's *Origin of Species*, for example, that makes it so persuasive is its wealth of detailed particularities. In his discussion of sexual selection, for example, Darwin provides the vivid example of the rooster:

> Sexual selection . . . depends, not on a struggle
> for existence, but on a struggle between the
> males for possession of the females; the re-
> sult is not death to the unsuccessful competi-
> tor, but few or no offspring. Sexual selection
> is, therefore, less rigorous than natural selec-
> tion. Generally, the most vigorous males,
> those best fitted for their places in nature, will
> leave most progeny. But in many cases, vic-
> tory will depend not on general vigour, but
> on having special weapons, confined to the
> male sex. A hornless stag or spurless cock
> would have poor chance of leaving offspring.
> Sexual selection by always allowing the victor
> to breed might surely give indomitable cour-
> age, length to the spur, and strength to the
> wing to strike in the spurred leg, as well as
> the brutal cock-fighter, who knows well that

he can improve his breed by careful selection
of the best cocks. (136)

Such detailed particulars throughout the work "add
up" to the principle of evolution, even though Darwin himself did not know what a gene was and could
not himself explain how evolution occurred. There
is no need to assume that induction ever operates
without deduction, though, that there is "science
without theory"; that is simply not true. In fact, there
are fine instances of deduction in the *Origin of Species*
that clearly preceded rather than followed his inves-
tigations, perhaps the most important of which is
that Darwin believed that, "whilst this planet has
gone cycling on according to the fixed law of gravity, from so simple a beginning endless forms most
beautiful and most wonderful have been, and are
being, evolved" (460), it is possible to discover "the
laws impressed on matter by the Creator" (458).
What makes empiricism true is not that there is any
innocent perception; what makes empiricism true
is that it is a method by which one can test principles against the actual world. That test requires
patience and honesty, but, because it relies upon
what we can actually "see," it is easier than tests that
are, in essence, not empirical, but rational. If one
lists facts and then, through the process of induction, generalizes about those facts, then one will
"see" whether or not the facts do indeed support
the proposition. If you move not from particular to
principle but from principle to principle, though,

the relationship will be harder to see. As Richard Weaver puts it in *A Rhetoric and Composition Handbook*, "By [deduction] propositions are established not . . . by direct observation of facts, but by reference to other already established propositions" (118). Whereas science is the study of observable phenomena and the rules that make such phenomena intelligible, logic is the study of propositions and the way one proposition refers to another. In rhetoric, one uses induction like a scientist and deduction like a logician. As we will see, rhetorical induction proceeds through examples, while rhetorical deduction proceeds through enthymemes.

[2.7]   Propositions refer to one another in different ways, and logical syllogisms are the established forms of such reference. There are three kinds of syllogism—the categorical, the hypothetical, and the disjunctive. Each has three propositions: the major premise, the minor premise, and the conclusion. We differentiate the three kinds by the nature of the premises and the form of the relationship between and among them. Each kind of syllogism is in danger of a specific fallacy. The categorical syllogism is the most famous kind of syllogism. Anyone with any interest in philosophy at all will recognize the following syllogism: "All people are mortal; Socrates is a person; therefore, Socrates is mortal." This is, in fact, a categorical syllogism. The major premise is categorical: all things in category X have the at-

tribute Y. So, too, is the minor: A is in category X.
The conclusion then follows by logical necessity: A
must have the attribute Y that all X's have. We can
chart this easily enough:

Major premise:	All X are Y.
Minor premise:	A is X.
Conclusion:	Therefore, A is Y.

One can qualify the categorical syllogism by quali-
fying the major premise. Perhaps only some X are Y;
perhaps no X are Y; perhaps, indeed, some X are not
Y. You get the idea. The point is this: categorical syllogisms assume that things belong to categories or
groups. The second paragraph of Jefferson's Declaration of Independence is a marvel of logic, and it
begins with categorical propositions:

> We hold these truths to be self-evident: that
> all men are created equal; that they are en-
> dowed by their creator with inherent and in-
> alienable rights; that among these are life, lib-
> erty and the pursuit of happiness; that to se-
> cure these rights, governments are instituted
> among men, deriving their just powers from
> the governed. . . . (19)

All people are equal in the rights they have; governments, if they *are* governments, secure those rights
for those who are sovereign, the governed. Now
Jefferson is too fine a rhetor to fill in the full syllo-

gism: All men are created equal; you, Reader, and I are men; therefore, we are equal. Rhetoric is not mathematics: Rhetors leave out whatever premises a reader or listener can supply; even so, their elliptical syllogisms—called enthymemes—are nonetheless often enough categorical, hypothetical, and/or disjunctive. Now the category of "man" has itself been a term of argument; after all, Jefferson understood that the slaves he owned—because, as men, equal to him—ought to have had their rights secured by the very government that instead enslaved them. Historically, the principles of American politics are categorical and, therefore, universal, even if their execution has been selective and, therefore, elitist. Jefferson founded an inconsistent nation even as he fashioned a consistent argument. The inherent contradiction within American slavery was both a shame and a promise; after all, only a nation committed to equality would be logically and morally compelled to abolish the institution of slavery. And that commitment turns out to be an assumption about government, that the essential end of government is the security of rights. A government *is* one, in fact, only when it fulfills that teleological goal; otherwise, it falls into another category, the category of tyranny.

[2.8] Jefferson is not finished, though; he is, one must remember, arguing for revolution, and he completes his list of self-evident truths with two arguments, one hypothetical and another disjunctive:

> ... whenever any form of government becomes
> destructive of these ends, it is the right of the
> people to alter and abolish it, and to institute
> new government, laying its foundation on
> such principles, and organizing its powers in
> such form, as to them shall seem most likely
> to effect their safety and happiness. (19)

Jefferson's case is both hypothetical and disjunctive, as we well see once we define the hypothetical and disjunctive syllogisms. Where the categorical syllogism recognizes or invents groups, the hypothetical imagines conditions, then reasons about them:

Major premise:	If P, then Q.
Minor premise:	P.
Conclusion:	Therefore, Q.

Where the hypothetical syllogism imagines conditions, the disjunctive offers exclusive alternatives and then argues against one and for the other:

Major premise:	Either A, or B
Minor premise:	Not A.
Conclusion:	Therefore, B.

Jefferson combines both into a single graceful case. He argues that "whenever" or if X, then either A or B: if a government does not secure the rights of the governed, the people must either "alter" or "abolish" said government and found a reformed or new government that will. Jefferson explains later that the colonists have "petitioned" to alter the government and have been ignored: If X, then either A or B; not A; therefore, B. The only question that remains is this: Is the condition of the conditional syllogism, the imagined possibility of tyranny, in fact real? All Jefferson must do rhetorically from that point on is demonstrate British tyranny, and it is to that end that he submits the "facts" of tyranny to "a candid world," his list of George III's nasty crimes (20–22), the empirical basis for the judgment that the tyranny was not simply hypothetical. Jefferson's concise deduction is followed by ample induction to prove to those who could observe that a "prince whose character is thus marked by every act which may define a tyrant is unfit to be the ruler of a free people" (22). Like Darwin, Jefferson exploits both principles and particularities.

[2.9]   The enthymeme and the example constitute the fundamental proofs in rhetoric, but their requirements for persuasiveness are not as strict as those for their counterparts in logic and science. An enthymeme—literally, the "in-the-mind" argument—leaves premises out because they can be supplied by the reader; a rhetorical example need not be as exhaustive as a scientific one. Aristotle goes so far in the *Rhetoric* as to call the enthymeme the substance of rhetoric, the fundamental proof that structures any suasion (1.1.3). Why? Because we are always leaving premises unwritten when we write. Since the writer and the reader share a common understanding of so many things, supplying them all in any proof would be tedious. Taken far enough, such pedantry would make it impossible to achieve anything rhetorically. Although enthymemes must meet the strictest standards of logic once their premises are brought to light, such proofs need not state all that may be inferred. Likewise, the requirement of an exhaustive collection of examples in science is relaxed in rhetoric. Frequently, one example will do. Of course, it must be representative; otherwise, a counter-example will crush you. Even so, one vividly drawn example will be more persuasive than a catalogue of less vivid ones. Enthymemes and examples are compelling in their very economy.

[2.10] We judge the force of propositions, then, not only by their empirical support, but also by their rational coherence. Jefferson might have confused his categories: Must a government secure rights to be a government? Plato might not think so, believing Jefferson to be guilty of equivocating, shifting between two different meanings of the same term "government," at times meaning any government, at times meaning one particular form of it, the democratic. Jefferson might have fallaciously confused the consequence of rebellion for the antecedent of tyranny: Do people rebel without the presence of tyranny? Looters certainly do. Jefferson might have assumed that there were only two alternatives when there were more, the either-or fallacy: Are peaceful petition and violent rebellion the only two possible responses to tyranny? Martin Luther King Jr. did not believe so. But the readers whose souls he was leading did believe that England was tyrannizing them, that they had a right to alter or abolish such a tyranny, and that, having petitioned to alter it long enough, it was time to shoot some Redcoats and harass their sympathizers. The logic of the argument was persuasive: America became a democracy.

[2.11] And democracy was what the Federalists wanted a decade later to refine. Madison does so in *Federalist* 10 by employing not only the syllogisms of logic, but also the topics of invention. The root of "topic" is the Greek word *topos*, "a location"; a topic of invention is a territory or place of invention. There are five common topics of invention: definition, comparison, relationship, circumstance, and testimony. The five can be employed as questions to help a writer invent arguments about X:

> 1. *Can I define X*: What are its general and specific characteristics?
>
> 2. *Can I compare X and Y*: How and to what degree are they alike or different?

3. *What is the relationship between X and Y*: cause and effect, or antecedent and consequence, or contraries, or contradictions?

4. *What are the circumstances of X*: impossible, possible, improbable, probable, certain?

5. *Is there any testimony to support argument about X*: an authority, a testimonial, a statistic, a maxim, a law, and/or a precedent or example?

Memorize these questions; then, when writing, draw upon them. We will examine in detail only three of the topics of invention: definition, comparison, and relationship. Each topic of invention, or "location of discovery," enables the writer to prove through argument the case being prosecuted, the thesis *[2.3]*. Let's take up each and examine Madison's qualification of Jefferson's case.

[2.12] Definition first. All formal definitions have two parts: The first part is the *genus* the object falls within; the second, the *differentiae* that distinguish the object from other, different objects that fall into the same genus. When Madison defines "pure democracy" as "a society consisting of a small number of citizens, who assemble and administer the government in person" (126), he posits the genus of any regime as a governed society; because societies differ in the mode of such government, though, he designates democracy's small size and direct rule as differentiating characteristics. Definitions are not a-rhetorical, though; they are *stipulative*. Unlike dictionary definitions, which explain how a word is used, stipulative definitions argue that a word ought to mean what the rhetor says it does. Such definitions stipulate meaning. Madison is arguing against democracy, in the strict sense of the word, because he believes that republicanism is a better form of government for the states. Thus, when he emphasizes the smallness of pure democracy, he is preparing the reader for his case that the nation is already too big for direct administration. My point is not to criticize his definition; it is simply to acknowledge that definitions are arguments. After all, even mathematical definitions are debatable. Euclid's definition of a "line" in his *Elements* as "breadthless length," for example, is rejected by Aristotle in *De anima*, where he defines it instead as "a point by its motion" (153; quoted 159). When employing the topic of definition, be sure to avoid equivocation; once you define your term, maintain its meaning throughout; otherwise, what you prove of it in one place will not be compelling in another. Major yet unclear terms weaken most student writing.

[2.13] Definitions often prepare a reader for comparison. One of the best ways to compare and contrast two objects is to argue that they share a *genus* but do not share all of the same *differentiae*. Madison is arguing against democracy and for republicanism. To do so, he must compare them:

> The two great points of difference between a democracy and a republic are: first, the delegation of the government, in the latter, to a small number of citizens elected by the rest; secondly, the greater number of citizens, and greater sphere of country over which the latter may be extended. (123)

Because Madison believes that delegation ensures a more reasonable deliberation—the few refining the intellectual and emotional temper of the many—he prefers republicanism. Notice that his entire case depends upon a differentiation between the two forms of government being compared. Indeed, it turns out that republicanism can better cure the polity of faction, according to Madison.

[2.14] After defining faction—"a number of citizens, whether amounting to a majority or minority of the whole, who are united and actuated by some common impulse or passion, or of interest, adverse to the rights of other citizens or to the permanent and aggregate interests of the community" (123)—he develops his case by employing the common topic of relationship, the most important of which is cause and effect. The topic of causality relates X and Y causally: X is cause or effect of Y. It is important to remember that causality must be explained, not simply assumed. Many things follow other things without being their effects. (The *post hoc, ergo propter hoc* fallacy—"after-this-therefore-because-of-this"—can result if one forgets this.) What causes "faction"? Two causes: liberty and intellectual diversity. As he explains, "There are two methods of removing the causes of faction: the one, by destroying the liberty which is essential to its existence; the other, by giving every citizen the same opinions, the same passions, the same interests." Madison approves of neither choice, so he argues that the best way to control the effects of what is simply part of our nature is republican government. Madison's use of the topics of definition, comparison, and relation is exemplary.

[2.15] Madison's paper is not in the least academic; after all, he, Hamilton, and Jay were writing a newspaper column. Academic writing relies upon yet another topic, testimony, as its central form of evidence, the testimony of an authority in research or that of the text in explication. Whenever you try to persuade your reader to believe your proposition about the text under investigation, you must persuade your reader that the proposition accords with the work, that it explicates and makes intelligible both the particularities of the text's parts and its whole being. You must be able to substantiate your ideas by disclosing their presence in the text, persuading the text to testify on behalf of your argument. To explicate the text, you must analyze part of the text and synthesize its parts with each other. Why? Because if you don't, the reader you are leading is under no intellectual obligation to believe you. Writing about texts, especially literary ones, demands that you measure your ideas by their capacity to fit the text. This is not easy, because the textual world is itself so very complex and full that it is not easy to be wise about it. Criticism is like prudence, or practical wisdom, in this regard. As Aristotle explains in the *Nicomachean Ethics*, "Nor is prudence a knowledge of general principles only; it must also take into account particular facts" (7.7.7). That "taking-into-account" of the facts demands a more flexible perception than you might yet have. The humanities sharpen your intellect and imagination by asking you to fashion arguments about works that elude facile points. To create an argument that will be just to a fine text demands a form of attention during your reading that is, at first, alien. As Thoreau argues in *Walden*,

> To read well, that is, to read true books in a true spirit, is a noble exercise, and one that will task the reader more than any exercise which the customs of the day esteem. It requires a training such as the athletes underwent, the steady intention almost of the whole life to this object. Books must be read as deliberately and as reservedly as they were written. (91–92)

This is, of course, quite a demand, an ideal you may not be able to achieve during every reading you do, but it must remain your ideal if you are to be persuasive about these books. To meet the demands of analysis and synthesis is to achieve this ideal. Analysis dives down into a part of the text; synthesis swims across the whole of it.

[2.16] First, analysis: analysis demands that you untie the textual knot, showing the truth of your argument within the passage itself. There is a three-step formula for analysis which, once mastered, can become more than a formula: Articulate your point; quote a passage—long or short—that supports that point; then relate point and passage and explore. Imagine that you are writing an essay about Book 1 of the *Iliad*, Homer's other epic, especially the episode in which Athena arrives during the argument between Achilleus and Agamemnon and stops Achilleus from murdering the leader by offering him counsel, and imagine that you want to argue that Athena is a metaphor for Achilleus's judgment. Following the above pattern, you might write a paragraph like this:

> Athena is Achilleus's practical judgment. It is when he deliberates about either killing Agamemnon for dishonoring him or calming himself that she appears to him: "Now as he weighed in mind and spirit these two courses

/ and was drawing from its scabbard the great sword, Athene descended from the sky" (1.193–95). She arrives "as" he deliberates, her descent a sign of an instant of calm reflection before action. This explains why no one else can see her (198–99): she is present to him alone because he alone is deliberating.

This paragraph is structured by means of the analysis formula. Most students make points; a few substantiate them with quotes; almost none, at first anyway, then explore the relationship between the two. It is in that third step, though, that one's perception of particularities becomes most discerning; it is in that step that one begins to say what may never have been said about the text. Analysis is a source of originality. Not all professors like the text actually quoted, by the way; your various audiences have, as you already know, different preferences *[1.5]*. In that case, refer to the passage without actually quoting it: "'It is when he deliberates about either killing Agamemnon for dishonoring him or calming himself that she appears to him' (1.193–95)." That lets the reader know you know the text, but keeps the passage itself out of the essay. Sometimes you may simply allude to the passage without providing any reference. As a general rule, then, cite any text that is essential to your major proof, but only refer or allude to any text that is not.

[2.17] The object of analysis is itself a whole made up of parts: Athena's exchange with Achilleus is one part or episode within the whole poem of the *Iliad*. When one fashions an argument about a text, one is trying to persuade one's reader to believe that the case will make sense not only of its parts, however, but also of its totality. Analysis requires synthesis; otherwise, the reader will suspect that the case is true locally but globally untrue, or at least unexplored. Synthesis places parts into a relationship with one another in order to provide a reading of the whole. Let's return to our hypothetical essay on Athena and see how both analysis and synthesis persuade:

> Athena is Achilleus's practical judgment. It is when he deliberates about either killing Agamemnon for dishonoring him or calming himself that she appears to him: "Now as he weighed in mind and spirit these two courses / and was drawing from its scabbard the great sword, Athene descended from the sky" (1.193–95). She arrives "as" he deliberates, her descent a sign of an instant of calm reflection before action. This explains why no one else can see her (198–99): she is present to him alone because he alone is deliberating. Athena never returns to assist Achilleus in the *Iliad*. It is clear from her prophecy that "[s]ome day three times over such shining gifts shall be given you / by reason of this outrage" (213–14) that she would have advised him to accept

Agamemnon's gifts in Book 9 had she been present. She is not. By Book 9, Achilleus's deliberations are missing a divine presence. He alone decides to remain away from the war; he alone brings about his tragedy, his practical judgment distorted by increasingly philosophical speculations about the purpose of human life. Athena does not rule over such speculations.

By placing one part—Book 1—in relation to another—Book 9—the writer synthesizes those parts into an argument about the whole. Aristotle argues in the *Poetics* that the soul of tragedy is its plot, and plot is the arrangement of episodes (1450a3-4); the Greek for "arrangement" is *synthesis.* When one examines any whole text, one must comprehend its total, not simply its partial being. To be persuasive about the argumentative subject *[2.3]*, one must discern the order of parts that constitute the whole. There is, of course, a danger that one will lose focus *[2.2]* if one begins to examine the entire meal and not just one of its dishes. This is a problem. Yet remember, in rhetoric, problems are resources. Only by recognizing, confronting, and triumphing over problems can one release the light of *logos*. Recognition, confrontation, and triumph entail revision *[5]*, a writing process whose product will be persuasive about the essence of the text, its plot.

[2.18] Focus, argument, the development of ideas, the explication of text: the demands of invention are extraordinary, but they are demands students can and should be expected to meet. Only high standards of evaluation disclose to the student what he or she needs to work on *[Appendix 2]*. Students are often suspicious of this line of reasoning and will think to themselves what they are far too pragmatic to say to their professors, "No one could do this; this isn't fair." Students need to read student work in order to realize that they are themselves capable of excellent writing. Before reading on, please first read Tommy Heyne's essay, "The Maturation of Telemachos" *[Appendix 1]*. I will examine the essay in this and the next two chapters, investigating first its invention, then its organization, and finally its style.

[2.19] The focus of the essay *[2.2]* is quite sharp, even though Mr. Heyne is trying to comprehend the whole of the *Odyssey*. His focus came from the essay prompt itself:

> In the *Poetics*, Aristotle argues that tragic poetry is a representation of a single action that is serious. Epic, of course, represents many various actions; even so, there will often be unity, even in and among all the various episodes, the poem held together by a single action. In the *Odyssey*, that action is the restora-

tion of a family and a polity. That restoration involves three related but distinct lives, though: Odysseus, Penelope, and Telemachos. In a four- to six-page essay (1000–1250 words) chart *one* of the three main characters and answer the following questions: What action does Homer represent that character as performing, and how does that action help restore the household and polity? Although you are not to lose sight of the other members of the family, your primary focus will be on your chosen character.

As with many prompts, this one is composed of questions, and it provides the scale which will determine focus *[2.2]*. Mr. Heyne maintains focus by means of a compelling thesis *[2.3]*: "Telemachos's maturation . . . is essential to the restoration of the Odyssean household and regime because Telemachos, once mature, is able to help Odysseus forcibly get rid of the suitors and because . . . he becomes a viable heir who will maintain the same high standards set by Laertes and Odysseus" (126). Notice that the thesis has two parts: The first is his subject, the character's maturation; the second is how this maturation helps restore the household. Each part answers a question in the prompt; both parts encompass the two parts of the poem he will investigate—the Telemachy of Books 1-4 and the Restoration of Books 13-24. (Notice that the only part of the text not addressed, Books 5-12, are those which represent Odysseus alone.) Mr. Heyne devel-

ops the thesis through the topic of definition
[2.12]—What is Telemachos's maturation?—in an examination of the young man's own odyssey. Though he has no single-sentence definition of "maturity," throughout he establishes its characteristics as active, authoritative, and self-sufficient. He defends his thesis with both analysis *[2.16]* and synthesis *[2.17]*. Providing evidence that, by the end of the poem, Telemachos is ready to govern lawlessness in Ithaca, he cites the character's highly significant lines: "I now notice all and know of it" (130). Throughout, the essay's textual evidence is strong. Mr. Heyne offers evidence for most of his points, and the essay's synthesis is especially mature, the writer's ability to discern relationships between and among episodes quite compelling. As pointed out earlier—by relating Books 1–4 to 13–24, Telemachos's maturation to his assistance of Odysseus in regaining and reunifying the kingdom—the essay discerns a principle of wholeness in the poem. The thesis is true both in particular detail and in harmonic whole. The essay's invention—what it says—does indeed release light, and that is the light that certainly led this reader.

[2.20] Rhetorical power, we can now see, is not something restricted to the great texts of the monumental past, a power one worships as somehow different from one's own small powers. After all, traditions teach us how to take our place in them, even sometimes how to argue against them. Essays informed by the art of rhetoric do not worship greatness; they try to exhibit it.

3

Organization:
The Desire for Design

[3.1] "Your ideas are very good, but your punctuation is weak": it is quite common for a high school teacher to write such a comment on an essay, revealing as it does the two-part model of composition that still commonly governs so many teachers. There is form and there is content. Indeed, many high school English teachers even used to employ a divided grade to mark just this distinction. There are two problems with this model. First, it often assumes that the two can be separated, that an essay whose grammar, punctuation, and spelling are embarrassing can still have "a good idea." How would the reader know? Teachers are far too lenient here. Can you imagine a CEO responding with so much understanding? "Your report is very interesting and you have several good ideas, but your sentences need a little work." Right. The second problem with the two-part model is that it ignores organization: because the Five-Paragraph Essay is often the *only* shape allowed, it can be treated as though it were the natural shape of all writing. That shape is a convenience for people who are reading and grading far too many essays, an organizational technique that has, indeed, some value early on in a student's rhetorical career: After all, it encourages students to imagine that their essay has a beginning, a middle, and an end; it allows students to organize their thoughts with ease; and it *is* easy to grade. Even so, its limitations are great. Its most powerful limitation is this: it supplies *one* shape to all arguments, regardless of their nature.

[3.2]   But the second part of rhetoric is a great deal more interesting and flexible than that. Because all made things are products of *tekhnê* or art, they have a shape. They have been shaped. The shaping power of the human imagination is one of its greatest attributes, a characteristic we may share with the divine, as understood in Judaism: As the God of the Hebrew Bible shaped his cosmos, we shape ours; as he made nature, we make culture. And the parts of any whole product of culture—including that marvel of art, the essay—must be arranged, disposed in an order that discloses not only a design, but also the design that the made thing ought to have. Let me be less cosmic. An essay's invention—what it has to say—will often have several potential organizational designs—orders in which it should say what it has to say. Ideally, organization comes out of invention, the design of the whole immanent within its argument. What does "immanent design" mean? After discussing the poem below, Andrew Marvell's "To His Coy Mistress," I will explain "immanent design." The rhetorical purpose of the poem is to seduce a lady who is, apparently, resisting the poet's sexual advances. Marvell's speaker is one of Darwin's "vigorous males," armed not with spur or wing, but with sophistry:

> Had we but world enough, and time,
> This coyness, lady, were no crime.
> We would sit down, and think which way
> To walk, and pass our long love's day.
> Thou by the Indian Ganges' side
> Shouldst rubies find; I by the tide
> Of Humber would complain. I would
> Love you ten years before the flood,
> And you should, if you please, refuse
> Till the conversion of the Jews.　　　　10
> My vegetable love should grow
> Vaster than empires and more slow;
> An hundred years should go to praise
> Thine eyes, and on thy forehead gaze;
> Two hundred to adore each breast;
> But thirty thousand to the rest;
> An age at least to every part,
> And the last should show your heart.
> For, lady, you deserve this state,
> Nor would I love at lower rate.　　　　20
> But at my back I always hear
> Time's winged chariot hurrying near;

And yonder all before us lie
Deserts of vast eternity.
Thy beauty shall no more be found;
Nor, in thy marble vault, shall sound
My echoing song; then worms shall try
That long-preserved virginity,
And your quaint honor turn to dust,
And into ashes all my lust.   30
The grave's a fine and private place
But none, I think, do there embrace.
Now, therefore, while the youthful hue
Sits on thy skin like morning dew,
And while thy willing soul transpires
At every pore with instant fires,
Now let us sport us while we may,
And now, like amorous birds of prey,
Rather at once our time devour
Than languish in his slow-chapped power.   40
Let us roll our strength and all
Our sweetness into one ball,
And tear our pleasures with rough strife
Through the iron gates of life:
Thus, though we cannot make our sun
Stand still, yet we will make him run.

The poem is, in fact, a hypothetical syllogism. Did you notice? It begins with the hypothesis—If A, then B—then negates A and concludes with -B:

> Major Premise: If we were immortal, then I would court you at leisure.

| Minor Premise: | We are not immortal. |
| Conclusion: | Therefore, I cannot court you at leisure; let's just do it. |

Let's leave to the side the question of the logical strength of the syllogism and instead focus on the poem's overall design. Its parts are immanent within its argument; that is, the order of the parts come from the syllogism itself: Part I establishes the major premise; Part II, the minor; and Part III, the conclusion. In fact, the poem's invention and organization are difficult to cut asunder because Marvell arranges the proofs in the order most commonly employed for hypothetical reasoning: Part I encompasses lines 1–20; II, 21–32; and III, 33–46. The poem need not have been ordered thus, and it would be an excellent exercise to try other arrangements; even so, the shape is certainly one of the stronger immanent shapes within Marvell's case to the lady, and much of the poem's humor results from a highly rational form housing such a passionate argument. An "immanent design," then, is a shape which dwells within the work, the one most suitable to the purpose of that work. Ideally, the organizational principle of your essay will be the one that dwells immanently within it.

[3.3]   But we are not always ideal beings. This chapter will offer a specific shape, much more flexible than the Five-Paragraph Essay, much less so than the Immanent-Design Essay. You should eventually be capable of the Immanent-Design Essay, but it is a sophisticated arrangement, one that becomes easier as your rhetorical powers mature; meanwhile, I will emphasize a particular shape, the design of the Classical Oration, slightly modified. This design is, in fact, a formula, one that—having been mastered—can, however, be transformed, remade to suit your argument; this inherited design should lead to new designs, the ones you create in order to do justice to the varied arguments you release. The Classical Oration has six parts: Part I is the introduction; Part II, the statement of circumstance; Part III, the outline; Part IV, the proof; Part V, the refutation; and Part VI, the conclusion. The introduction, statement and outline are the essay's beginning; its proof and refutation are its middle; and its conclusion is its end. An introduction leads the reader into the essay, establishing the essay's subject, its focus, and— often, but not always—its argument *[2.2–2.3]*. The statement of circumstance is background the reader needs to situate the argument. The outline delineates the parts of the proof and refutation so the reader knows, before beginning, the shape of the essay's body. Your proof is your argument proper, the section in which you demonstrate the truth of the argument through both development *[2.4–2.14]* and explication *[2.15–2.17]*; your refutation is your counter-argument, the section in which you imagine and critique arguments other than your own in order to strengthen your case. And the conclusion completes the essay by leading the reader out of the essay. These parts are not necessarily paragraphs; any one of the parts may be composed of more than one paragraph. To examine each part in greater detail, let the order of the parts dictate the order of the presentation.

[3.4] Beginnings and endings are difficult because one must determine how far back to begin and how far forward to end. Now, one need not usually begin with the Creation, nor end with the Apocalypse. An introduction has two purposes: it lets the reader know what your rhetorical purpose is, and it persuades the reader that your essay is worth reading. First, the introduction determines the essay's subject, focus, and—usually—argument. The most common way to achieve all three is the "funnel-in" introduction in which you begin with the general subject matter, limit the focus, and state your thesis. Suppose one were writing an essay on the leadership of Agamemnon in the *Iliad*. Your introduction might look like this:

> Leadership requires patience, practical wisdom, and courage. Of the three, practical wisdom is the most important, and—as we see in Book 1 of Homer's *Iliad*—that is the attribute Agamemnon lacks. Agamemnon is not a good leader because he is rash in his judgments.

The "funnel-in" introduction is solid, but it is not the only way to begin an essay. Relying upon a nineteenth-century rhetorician, Richard Whately, Edward Corbett offers five other possibilities: The "inquisitive" introduction; the "paradoxical"; the "corrective"; the "preparatory"; and the "narrative." Let's take up each and invent an introduction for this imaginary essay by means of its principles. The "inquisitive" introduction leads the reader into the essay by persuading him or her that the subject is a question to be explored (283):

> Because we are associative creatures, we continually influence others. Everyone, then, is a kind of leader; as a consequence, the ethical life requires that one understand and exercise good leadership. How does one become a good leader? By fulfilling all three of its requirements: patience, practical wisdom, and courage. To be without one of the requirements is to be a poor leader. As we see in Book 1 of Homer's *Iliad*, Agamemnon is a poor leader because, although he is indeed courageous, he is also both impatient and rash. He proves to be a negative example for the reader who wants to understand leadership.

The "paradoxical" introduction leads the reader into the essay by persuading him or her that, although your case seems improbable, it is actually true (284):

Agamemnon is not a very sympathetic character in Book 1 of Homer's *Iliad* in great part because he appears, at first, to be so rash that his decisions seem to be those of a poor leader; as a consequence, it is difficult to persuade readers of the poem that he is, in fact, a good leader. Agamemnon is a good leader, though, because the good leader, although he or she must have practical wisdom, must often decide and act very quickly. Rashness is often a virtue of good rulers. Agamemnon is a good leader because he acts swiftly in the face of challenges to his authority.

The "corrective" introduction persuades the reader that the subject has not been addressed adequately yet, an inadequacy the essay will remedy (284):

Most readers believe that Agamemnon is responsible for the quarrel he and Achilleus enter at the beginning of Book I of Homer's *Iliad*, arguing that, because the political ruler dishonors the powerful warrior, he is ultimately responsible for the quarrel. This is not the case. Achilleus, because he attempts to usurp Agamemnon's political role by calling the Assembly, is responsible for the quarrel. Although the scepter may be passed to any, only one man ought to hold it first, and that man, "lord of men," is Agamemnon.

The "preparatory" introduction persuades the reader that some unusual feature of your case is worth attending to (285):

> Readers of Books 1 and 2 in the *Iliad* base their deliberations over Agamemnon's leadership on the Assembly in Book 1 where he quarrels with Achilleus. I would like to base mine on the Assembly in Book 2 where he tests the men. Agamemnon is not a good leader because he does not know what the men he is leading think and feel about their situation; as a consequence, in both Books 1 and 2, he misreads them, asking of them what he should not.

The "narrative" introduction persuades the reader by providing narrative detail that leads to the subject at hand (286):

> After nine days of plague, a plague that is devastating the troops, Achilleus, not Agamemnon, calls an assembly to deliberate the source of Apollo's anger. Because we have already seen Agamemnon's imprudent treatment of Apollo's priest, the priest's prayer to Apollo for vengeance, and Apollo's descent from Olympus to disease the Greeks, we know that Homer wants us to attend to Agamemnon's silence during the opening of the Assembly, an assembly that quite quickly and directly, but not explicitly, is a challenge to his authority, a challenge to which he will

respond with characteristic rashness. Agamemnon is not a good leader because his practical wisdom is deficient.

Each of the introductions leads into its respective, imaginary essay by interesting the reader in the subject at hand; each does so differently. Your audience, remember, will be reading many essays on the same select number of prompts. Variety pleases. And a pleased reader is more attentive to an argument than a bored one, more likely convinced that the time spent inside the cosmos of your essay will be worth the time. It isn't only lovers who hear Time's winged chariot hurrying near. A writer who fulfills his or her obligation to please the reader with variety persuades the reader that the reading is time well spent making the sun run.

[3.5] We now come to two common questions. First: How does one know which introduction to employ? The ultimate principle is immanence: use the type that suits your argument. If you are arguing something unusual, some case nowhere even hinted at in class discussion, you may want to prepare the reader for it. If you are planning on correcting your professor's reading of the text, let him or her know in the introduction what to expect. There is no part of the art of rhetoric which can be reduced to a simple formula, even if there are indeed formulae to be learned. Remember: Rhetoric is a power of the mind; it is not a program *[1.3]*. This intellectual power demands attention to the rhetorical contingencies of the situation *[1.5]*. Rhetorical attention is called for during invention, organization, and style. You may want to experiment; those experiments ought to be governed whenever possible, though, by your rhetorical situation. The second common question is this: Should one include the thesis *[2.3]* in the introduction? Again, you will need to consult your rhetorical circumstances. Does your professor want it there? Some do. If the professor leaves it up to the writer, would a terminal thesis be persuasive? Generally, the more exploratory your essay, the more likely it will be that you will want to end on your argument rather than begin with it. If so, the body's shape should be exceptionally clear, so lucid the reader never suspects that you are hunting for a thesis, willing to shoot whatever darts from a bush as you wander through a dark wood of error and confusion. The temptation to do just that, a temptation increased with procrastination *[5]*, must be resisted; otherwise, the rhetorical community is diminished and professors will demand that every thesis come in the introduction in order to prevent thesis-hunting.

[3.6] The second part of the essay, the statement of circumstance, is also contingent. If your audience is already familiar with the circumstances of the case, you may exclude this part altogether, although your reader, even though he or she is familiar with them, may want you to demonstrate that *you* are. You are writing for teachers, after all. The statement of circumstance is an exposition of the case at hand; here, you narrate the central events, historical or fictional, define the important terms, and/or articulate the crucial questions. This can often be done in the introduction itself; indeed, if you read the examples above, you will see that each does in fact state the case. When writing about literary texts, remember to narrate only those circumstances that pertain to your argument; otherwise, you will be "retelling" the story rather than fashioning an argument about the story. Homer already wrote his poems. You don't need to.

[3.7] The third part of the Classical Oration is the outline. An outline is crucial for two reasons: First, it indicates that the writer actually understands the shape of the proof; second, it pleases most readers because it lets them know what design within the essay to expect, and, when that expectation is met—when the themes introduced in the symphony's opening are explored and developed in the order they were introduced—the reader experiences a harmony between expectation and fulfillment. The designer of the whole ought to know the design of the parts. Why? Because, when a reader discovers that the leader of his or her soul has the cosmic comprehension of design, he or she is more likely to yield to that soul-leadership. An outline tells the reader explicitly what the essay will do. Imagine that one wants to argue that Agamemnon is not a good leader. Perhaps the writer wants to define the good leader before deciding that Agamemnon is not one. The proof might consist of two parts: In the first, the writer defines the good leader; in the second, he or she argues that Agamemnon does not meet that standard. An outline for such an essay might look like this: "Let us define the good leader, then examine Agamemnon's poor leadership." It might look like this: "What is a good leader? Is Agamemnon a good leader?" It might look like this: "There are two parts to my case—a definition of the good leader and an examination of Agamemnon's leadership." The two proofs then follow in the order you mention them, and the body's shape, as a consequence, is articulated, leading to the cosmic harmony of fine design. If your reader does not enjoy such harmony or prefers a more subtle—"figure-it-out-as-you-go-along"—design, then employ one. Never, however, fail to comprehend what the overall shape of the body is. Even if your rhetorical judgment directs you not to disclose the shape to the reader, preferring to let him or her discover it, that shape should be there to be discovered. I personally distrust such secretiveness and have found that students who do not want to "give away" the design seldom actually have one. Clarity is not at all dull; indeed, little is as intellectually thrilling as lucid design.

[3.8] If the introduction, statement of circumstance, and outline constitute your "beginning," the proof and refutation constitute your "middle," the body of the essay. It is in the proof that you prove your argument; that proof will usually contain several proofs. There is only one question to answer about your proofs: How should I order them? I cannot provide a general answer to that question because the answer depends—as almost all answers in rhetoric do—on the contingencies of the situation, especially the nature of your argument. It is here that the Classical Oration demands exactly what the Immanent Design does: comprehension of potential shapes. Here again, invention and organization are intertwined. The design of the body can, of course, be founded on the nature of the development. If you develop your case with a syllogism, structure the body by means of the parts of the syllogism; if you employ a topic of invention, structure the body by means of the topic itself; if you explicate, structure the body by means of the two methods, analysis and synthesis. Let invention disclose design. Jefferson, for example, had to decide, during the composition of "The Declaration of Independence," whether to dispose the principles first or the particulars *[2.6–2.10]*: Which first, induction or deduction? Jefferson's overall design is this:

Part I   Introduction

Part II   Proof 1: Deductive Argument

Why does he design the body as he does? One way to answer this question is to imagine another shape. Might Jefferson have first catalogued his facts, then supplied his principles? He might have, but it would be less effective. Why? Because the reader only sees the nature of those facts if he or she understands the principles; that is, the tyrannical essence of the oppressions has its full significance for the reader because he or she sees that they distort the very end of government that presumably justifies them. Why does the reader actually *see* that? Because Jefferson's second paragraph prepares the reader to see it. Examining the contingencies of his rhetorical situation, Jefferson discovered the best available means of persuasion by discerning within the nature of his argument the best available design. Shape itself has persuasive force, the design of the intellectual and imaginative territory leading us through the parts that make up its cosmos.

[3.9]   Arguments presuppose counter-arguments. Because propositions concern subjects about which reasonable people can disagree—otherwise, there would be no argument—different rhetors will declare different propositions about the same subject at hand. Controversy is built into human association. As a consequence, the rhetor must not only develop his or her own argument, but also imagine and refute counter-arguments if he or she is to be persuasive. Students do not, at first, believe this argument, convinced instead that encountering arguments other than their own will weaken, not strengthen, their case. There is no need to worry. One must invent arguments other than one's own and refute them, not simply to score points against an opponent, but rather to investigate the nature of the subject at hand. If you argue that Agamemnon is a poor leader, you must weigh the arguments that he is a good one; if you argue that Achilleus, not Agamemnon, is the cause of the quarrel, you must weigh the arguments that it is Agamemnon, not Achilleus, who is the cause. And so on. There are only two questions concerning refutation. First, should one refute? Second, should one refute *before* or *after* one's proof? Let's take the first question first. Even if one will not explicitly refute, one should—during the invention process *[5.3]*—imagine counter-arguments to strengthen one's own. If your audience is hostile to, or even merely skeptical of, your case—if the professor reads the text differently, for example—you must refute; otherwise, your reader will supply the refutation. A "hostile" reader, by the way, is not someone hostile to the writer personally; it is someone who disagrees with the writer's argument. All rhetorical communities house diverse opinions, and all rhetors face hostile audiences, even when the polity is a rhetorical community of friends. Even friends have their disagreements, after all, and there is no need to fear opposition or to demonize one's opponents. As Socrates explains so often in the dialogues, he himself searches for opposition because it is only through refutation that one can clarify one's own ideas. The Greek term for Socratic questioning, *elenkhos*, actually means "refutation," and the interlocutors in the dialogues who fear refutation are those who are either too ignorant to desire correction or too proud to tolerate it when it occurs. Interestingly, those who respond to Socratic refutation with anger are almost always unethical. Callicles in Plato's *Gorgias* and Thrasymachus in his *Republic*, for example, both respond to Socratic interrogation with incivility, which is, of course, quite natural; after all, who *enjoys* being refuted, especially in front of other people? But it is a sign of the good rhetor, as it is of the good friend, that he or she is willing to learn from others in the community, even if the lesson is sometimes embarrassing. As he continually reminds us, Socrates does enjoy being refuted. Let him be our ideal. "But he is seldom if ever himself refuted," I hear my reader declare. True. That may be because Socrates spends so much of his time imagining the counter-arguments he must surmount to be persuasive.

[3.10] The second question concerning refutation is also difficult. Although the formula of the Classical Oration places refutation after proof, one must sometimes refute first. When? There are two situations when one ought to refute first, then prove. The first of these is when one's audience is so hostile to one's argument that one must weaken the reader's confidence in his or her own case before offering an alternative [1.5]. If your reader slights or distrusts poetry, for example, and you want to defend the poets against Plato's criticism of them in the *Republic*, you will probably want to refute first. The need to refute might be based not on audience, however, but on subject [1.5]. Thus, when there is a counterargument which will confuse the reader unless it is refuted first, refute it before proving your own case. If one's cosmos is Socratic, one must build refutation into its design. One's reader will discern that the maker of the cosmos is him or herself a Socrates. Nothing is more persuasive to an academic audience.

[3.11] The last part of the essay, its "end," is the conclusion. The pleasure of endings is caused by our desire for completion. Readers want even good essays to come to an end; after all, there are others in the set to read. They want poor ones to do so even more quickly. The most common form of conclusion is the summary. There are two rules concerning summaries: let them be accurate, and let them be brief. If a summary includes points not actually discussed in the essay, the reader will become confused; if the summary is verbose, impatient. The greater your essay's scale, the more likely your reader will appreciate summaries, both throughout the essay and in its conclusion. You need not conclude with a summary, however; instead, you may want to try another form of conclusion. You may want to introduce a new but related subject or argument that you believe is necessitated by your argument but are unable to demonstrate; you may want to move your reader emotionally; you may want to return to the beginning of the essay, concluding with an idea, image, or piece of narrative or text with which you opened the essay. Try summarizing, then employing one of these three techniques; eventually, try not summarizing. The first conclusion technique exploits the particular nature of conclusions. The conclusion allows something seldom allowed elsewhere: the writer may express an opinion without proving it. The reader, having been persuaded by your case, will allow you to disclose another case without supporting it; after all, this is the essay's end. If, for example, your essay on Agamemnon's leadership argues and demonstrates that, in Books 1 and 2, Agamemnon is not a good leader, you might want to conclude thus:

> Because he is rash, Agamemnon is without the patience required for practical wisdom; because he is unwise, he is a poor leader in the

opening books. Perhaps, however, his leadership evolves within the poem as a whole. By Book 9, he is willing to be persuaded by Nestor to appease Achilleus and to yield to his demands. It is too late by then, of course, because Achilleus refuses to be persuaded by the very honor he earlier demanded. That is a disaster, but it is one caused by Achilleus's metaphysical doubts, not Agamemnon's political errors. By the time Agamemnon becomes an adequate leader, it is too late.

Notice that the writer need not explore Book 9 or prove the point. The reader has an obligation to allow it. Of course, a reader would always prefer to allow a persuasive point, so the writer ought to end with a strong, if undemonstrated, assertion.

[3.12] The second conclusion technique calls upon an appeal we have not yet discussed. There are, you will remember, three appeals (logical, emotional, and ethical), yet we have emphasized the first to the exclusion of the second and third *[1.4]*. *Pathos* and *ethos* are legitimate appeals, but in academic discourse they are less persuasive. Even so, conclusions in academic essays may persuade through the emotional appeal. (We will return to *ethos* in the next chapter *[4.3]*.) An emotional appeal rouses a particular emotion appropriate to the subject, then directs it by describing the action or object that will arouse the emotion. If you want your reader to be angry at Agamemnon, then you might conclude by describing the callousness with which he dishonors Achilleus, the description itself igniting anger in the reader; if you want your reader to be angry at Odysseus, then you might conclude by describing his manipulation of Penelope long after its utility. Anger is an emotion of justice. As Aristotle explains in the *Rhetoric*, "Anger may be defined as a desire accompanied by pain, for a conspicuous revenge for a conspicuous slight at the hands of men who have no call to slight oneself or one's friends" (2.2.1). One is angered because some principle of justice that ought to be executed is not. As we see here, emotions are cognitive; they disclose beliefs, including rational ones. A successful emotional appeal must be experienced by the rhetor him or herself, and it must not be announced *as* an emotional appeal. To appeal to an emotion, one arouses and then directs the emotion or emotions appropriate to the subject matter, as we see in Dr. Martin Luther King Jr.'s "Letter from Birmingham Jail." One of the most logical suasions in the American canon, King's letter often appeals nonetheless to the reader's emotions—for example, in King's description of the actual details of segregation. He is refuting the argument that blacks should "wait" for their human and civil rights rather than demonstrate to attain them:

> Perhaps it is easy for those who have never felt the stinging darts of segregation to say,

"Wait." But when you have seen vicious mobs lynch your mothers and fathers at will and drown your brothers and sisters at whim; when you have seen hate-filled policemen curse, kick and even kill your black brothers and sisters; when you see the vast majority of your twenty million Negro brothers smothering in an airtight cage of poverty in the midst of an affluent society; when you suddenly find your tongue twisted and your speech stammering as you seek to explain to your six-year-old daughter why she can't go to the public amusement park that has been advertised on television, and see tears welling up in her eyes when she is told that Funtown is closed to colored children, and see ominous clouds of inferiority beginning to form in her little mental sky, and see her beginning to distort her personality by developing an unconscious bitterness toward white people; when you have to concoct an answer for a five-year-old son who is asking: "Daddy, why do white people treat colored people so mean?"; when you take a cross-country drive and find it necessary to sleep night after night in the uncomfortable corners of your automobile because no motel will accept you; when you are humiliated day in and day out by nagging signs reading "white" and "colored"; when your first name becomes "nigger," your middle name becomes "boy" (however old you are) and your last name becomes "John," and your wife and mother are never given the respected title

"Mrs."; when you are harried by day and haunted by night by the fact that you are a Negro, living constantly at tiptoe stance, never quite knowing what to expect next, and are plagued with inner fears and outer resentments; when you are forever fighting a degenerate sense of "nobodiness"—then you will understand why we find it difficult to wait. There comes a time when the cup of endurance runs over, and men are no longer willing to be plunged into the abyss of despair. I hope . . . you can understand our legitimate and unavoidable impatience. (346–47)

This catalogue of injustices great and small arouses several emotions, one of which is an anger that results from righteous indignation; it does so by describing those injustices in such a way that we experience them imaginatively and ourselves grow impatient. (I suspect the sentence itself is so long so that the reader will grow impatient with the sentence: "When will this sentence end?" If the reader is impatient with the sentence, the writer must certainly and justifiably be impatient with the injustices the sentence represents.) Such an emotional appeal is legitimate. Why? Because injustice ought to arouse anger. Those not angered are not responding rationally. Emotional appeals are often quite persuasive in conclusions.

[3.13] The third technique of conclusion is called the "tail-biting-snake" conclusion; in it, the writer retrieves some element of the introduction—an idea, image, or piece of narrative or text—and repeats and varies it. As T. S. Eliot would have it in *The Four Quartets*, we return to the beginning and know it for the first time. Why can you only know the beginning of an essay at the end? Because, if its cosmos is harmonious, we will have learned its principle of construction while reading. This is a moving experience. Imagine you are composing an essay about Achilleus's pride. You might open and close with his memorably recalcitrant line, "He will not persuade me" (9.345). The repetition will not be exact repetition, though, because, as Heraclitus would have it, one cannot step in the same river twice. The line will read differently, more deeply, after your proof concerning it, and it will persuade your reader that the essay's design is total, that the essay is a complete whole whose parts cohere so fully that one might wish to read it again, to return to the beginning one now knows for the first time. All the techniques discussed—summary, new idea, emotional appeal, repetition—should convince your reader that the parts cohere into a complete whole, that the essay's design is not only intelligible but also beautiful. Beauty characterizes all good designs. An essay can be deformed; fortunately, deformed essays can be revised.

[3.14] Introduction, statement of case, outline, proof, refutation, conclusion: the six parts of organization are, remember, parts, not necessarily paragraphs. Though students have often been taught that every paragraph must have a topic sentence, one sentence that distills the proof in the paragraph which is proving the thesis, that is not strictly true. What is essential is that the material in the paragraph support the argument. Whatever part a paragraph inhabits, it must be both unified and coherent; that is, it must represent one thing, and it must do so rationally. If a paragraph is not unified, divide it; if it is not coherent, reconsider it. Unity is often difficult to ascertain. If, for example, you discuss one idea, but present two examples of it, should that be one paragraph or three? It depends. Paragraphs are conventional: Journalistic paragraphs tend to be quite short; academic ones, long. One can test one's paragraphing by asking the following question: Do the divisions lead the reader through the world of the essay with ease? To achieve coherence, include transitions within the paragraph that disclose its design. (Each part of the whole essay—its parts, its paragraphs, and its sentences—must be designed.) Again, let invention dictate organization: if a paragraph is defining, for example, examine the defined thing's *genus*, then its *differentiae [2.12]*. Each method of invention will disclose a paragraph arrangement. And employ one of the following four techniques of transition within the paragraph: Repeat important terms; employ unambiguous pronoun references; number your points; join clauses with accurate subordinate conjunctions and conjunctive adverbs. (These techniques work as transitional devices *between* paragraphs as well.) The following paragraph employs all four techniques of transition to achieve coherence. The repetitions are bolded; the clear pronouns are italicized; the numbered points are capitalized; and the subordinate conjunctions and conjunctive adverbs are underlined:

> Agamemnon is not a good leader <u>because</u>, <u>although</u> *he* is courageous, *he* is rash. ***A good leader*** must be both ***courageous*** and deliberate. FIRST, the ***good leader*** must have the ***courage*** to act, <u>even if</u> that action will offend some of *his* or *her* people, and ***Agamemnon*** is certainly ***courageous***. ***The good leader***, <u>however</u>, must also be ***deliberate***, and this SECOND virtue is even more important than the FIRST. ***Agamemnon*** lacks *this* SECOND ***virtue***.

A reader will seldom notice these techniques when they are used well and left unmarked; instead, he or she will follow the coherent path, only noticing transitions when they don't work.

[3.15] A finely designed essay—one in which the beginning, the middle, and the end fit into a harmonious whole and the parts and paragraphs of each cohere—ensures that the reader discovers the essay's invention by traveling within its organization. Student essays, even those whose invention is powerful and whose style is crisp and correct, often fail to take into account design. Reread Mr. Heyne's essay on the *Odyssey [Appendix 1]*. Its eight paragraphs make up a beginning, a middle, and an end:

Paragraph 1:	Introduction
Paragraphs 2–7:	Proof
	Proof I (2–5): Telemachos's Maturity
	Proof II (6–7): Its Place in the Restoration
Paragraph 8:	Conclusion

The essay opens with an introduction *[3.4-5]* that combines the corrective and the paradoxical, leading us to see that it is not Odysseus, the major character, he will examine, but Telemachos. The interesting comparison between Telemachos and Hamlet prepares us to see that, unlike *Hamlet*, the *Odyssey* is not a tragedy. Though the essay does not supply an internal outline *[3.7]*, the design of its middle is informed by the thesis, Mr. Heyne first disclosing the young man's maturation, then proving that it is just that maturation which helps restore Ithaka. Each part of the thesis in the introduction thus supplies the essay's proof *[3.8]* with its two-part structure, each part then divided into paragraphs *[3.14]*. Notice that the arrangement is in accord with the narrative itself, allowing the writer to handle early material from the poem first, its later material second. He concludes with a "tail-biting-snake" close: after summarizing his case, he closes where he began. Throughout, the essay's design-principle is never in doubt, its principle of wholeness harmonizing the world of the essay.

[3.16] In the best work, the reader experiences the harmony of invention and organization that define cosmic fashioning, a harmony that results from discipline, as Corbett explains, "a discipline that trains the student in the judicious selection and use of available means to the desired end" (338). Meaning is not only discovered through invention; it is also made through organization. The reader of a work that both discovers and makes will experience something unusual but persuasive—the pleasure that Stephen Booth describes in *An Essay on Shakespeare's Sonnets*: "Art comforts the spirit by presenting experience selected and organized in such a way as to exhibit the sense of pattern that the human mind tries to perceive in all of experience" (60). The selections of design exhibit patterns not otherwise perceived. Essays, like poems or foundings, are cosmic exhibits of the patterned truth your reader desires. To lead that reader's soul, you must know how to satisfy that desire.

4

Style:

Words and Sentences

[4.1]   If invention concerns "what" and organization concerns "in what order," then style concerns
"how." One's ordered case must be carried by one's
written prose, one's style. And, in the classical rhetorical tradition, style is made up of words and sentences, or diction and periods. One of the chief human glories is language itself, our capacity to name
the objects, actions, and relationships within our
world, and then to arrange such names into predications. Richard Weaver, you will remember from
Chapter 1, argues that the capacity to fashion sentences is a wondrous, even terrible power: "The liberty to impose this formal unity is a liberty to handle
the world, to remake it, if only a little, and to hand
it to others in a shape which may influence their
actions." To shape one's invented, disposed reflections upon an idea, an event, a text, or an artifact is
to handle it, remake it, if only a little, and hand it to
others in a shape that may influence their own re-

flections and actions. A rhetor must be articulate if he or she is to be a leader of souls. This may sound too elevated to be true. Students often think of style, when they think of it at all, as grammatical and punctuational correctness, and indeed, a good style must command both grammar and punctuation. It must possess more than such correctness, however. If it is to be a soul-leading style, its diction must be appropriate, precise, concise, and vivid; its periods must be varied in both length and pattern; and its figures of speech must be original. To handle one's subject articulately is to achieve the grace that attends all true language. After exploring the three styles of prose and their influence upon the rhetor's *ethos*, this chapter will address both diction and the period.

[4.2]   According to the authors of *Prose Style*, prose style comes in three forms—high, low, and middle. "The High Style aims at loftiness and grandeur" (3), and its identifying characteristics are an elevated diction and an elaborate syntax; the Low Style is "as plain and ordinary as the wording of casual conversation" (7), and its identifying characteristics are a familiar, even colloquial diction and a simple, casual syntax; the Middle Style, as its name suggests, lies in between the other two. Samuel Johnson, for example, writes in the High Style. Here, in his "Preface to *A Dictionary of the English Language*," the first major English dictionary, Johnson explains the difficulties of defining words:

> To interpret a language by itself is very difficult; many words cannot be explained by synonyms, because the idea signified by them has not more than one appellation; nor by paraphrase, because simple ideas cannot be described. When the nature of things is unknown, or the notion settled and indefinite, and various in various minds, the words by which such notions are conveyed, or such things described, will be ambiguous and perplexed. And such is the fate of hapless lexicography, that not only darkness, but light, impedes and distresses it; things may be not only too little, but too much known, to be happily illustrated. To explain requires the use of terms less abstruse than that which is to be explained, and such terms cannot always be found; for as nothing can be proved but by supposing something intuitively known, and evident without proof, so nothing can be defined but by the use of words too plain to admit a definition. (244–45)

This is fine prose, but its diction and syntax are more elevated than contemporary taste would appreciate. Though its diction is superb, "appellation" and "abstruse" would impress a contemporary reader as precious; though Johnson's syntax is one of the marvels of the English language, its complexities would chastise a contemporary reader with their difficulty. This prose is beautifully lucid, yet its pleasures require exercise to breathe at such an elevation. The Low Style is the High's opposite. When he invents prose for his dramatized narrator in *The Adventures of Huckleberry Finn*, Mark Twain writes in the Low Style, as one sees in the novel's memorable opening:

> You don't know about me, without you have read a book by the name of "The Adventures of Tom Sawyer," but that ain't no matter. That book was made by Mr. Mark Twain, and he told the truth, mainly. There was things he stretched, but mainly he told the truth. That is nothing. I never seen anybody but lied, one time or another, without it was Aunt Polly, or the widow, or maybe Mary. (27)

The diction here is plain, even colloquial, the syntax simple and coordinated. The prose is frequently incorrect. Though one of the best styles in all of American fiction, it is certainly too low, as Johnson's may be too high, for academic purposes. Notice, though, that their styles are perfect for their own rhetorical purposes. (For entertainment, imagine Huck writing Johnson's "Preface" and Johnson, the *Adventures*.) Academic prose ought to be in the Middle Style, tending toward, without becoming, the High, depending upon your audience *[1.5]*. Most professors have a taste for the High Style, though even they tire of it rather quickly. What, then, is the Middle Style?

> Middle Style occasionally borrows from High and Low—a few erudite words from the one, a few colloquialisms from the other. But mostly it uses words peculiar to neither extreme, words familiar to the general reader but not colloquial. It conveys the image of a writer who is intelligent but not pretentious, well educated but not pedantic, and able to relax without becoming slack or slovenly. (10)

The Middle Style, a mean between High and Low, requires appropriate, clear, and vivid diction without either grandiloquence or vulgarity, and it also requires appropriate, clear, and varied periods without excessive subordination or reductive simplicity. Mr. Heyne's prose is firmly in the Middle Style: "After his odyssey, Telemachus generally acts as a man, though he is still learning." Like all of us Middle Stylers, Mr. Heyne is somewhere between Johnson and Huck.

[4.3]   Notice that the Middle Style itself discloses *ethos*, the appeal to the rhetor's character as it reveals itself in the text itself. Remember that there are three appeals in rhetoric: the logical *[2.4]*, the emotional *[3.12]*, and the ethical. One's *ethos* is the person you appear to be *in your writing*, according to

Corbett, "the persuasive value" residing in "the speaker's or writer's character" (80), character that must possess intelligence, morality, and good nature to be persuasive. Perhaps no single feature of your writing affects your *ethos* as a student as much as style, so students whose grammar and punctuation are confused appear to be subliterate to their literate audience, even if they are not. Let me give just one example. Suppose you are reading the following sentence from an essay on the *Iliad*: "This fight between Agamoron and Akilles are stupid, they shoud just let it go." What is your impression of the writer? This is someone who appears, from the sentence alone, to be subliterate. The sentence is incorrect and colloquial: Its verb does not agree with its subject; the comma between its two clauses creates a comma splice; both simple words and the characters' names are accidentally but amusingly misspelled; and the diction is conversational. If Curious George had a computer, he would write prose like this. Rhetorically, it does not matter that the writer is not a Curious George. Because *ethos* is the writer as he or she appears in the writing itself. It will not be persuasive to say, "I have trouble with spelling"; for one thing, you shouldn't, and for another, you should know how to use your spell-check and dictionary. Nor will it be persuasive to say, "I know what I'm thinking; I just can't express it," because language and thought cannot be separated. After all, with what have you been all along inventing, if not diction and periods?

[4.4]   Diction is the single most difficult faculty to teach young writers because it simply takes time to gather a large enough vocabulary to allow wise word choice. Let me caution you about the standard remedy to this deficiency: A thesaurus seldom works unless used with a good dictionary; two words seldom, if ever, mean *exactly* the same thing. A thing may indeed have any number of words orbiting it, but each word will disclose—if not denotatively, then certainly connotatively—a distinct aspect of the thing. (A word's denotation is what it means in fact; its connotation, what it means by association. A "statesman" and a "politician" may in fact be the same, but we associate the former with wisdom and self-sacrifice and the latter with their opposites.) Imagine writing an essay for a class in philosophy about Aristotle's conception of *eudaimonia*, or "happiness," in the *Nicomachean Ethics*. You tire of employing the term "happiness" repeatedly, so you search your thesaurus. Beware! There are any number of synonyms for "happiness," yet each refracts the idea in a slightly different way, as one sees in the mini-essay on the term and its synonyms in *The Scribner-Bantam English Dictionary*:

> *Pleasure*, the opposite of pain, is an agreeable emotion covering all degrees of the feeling. *Enjoyment* is the taking or experiencing of *pleasure*. *Happiness* is a state of glowing *pleasure*, of being radiantly contented with one's lot. *Joy* is vivid, profound, demonstrative, and, be-

cause of its intensity, often transient. *Gladness*, though as strong as *joy*, is more serene and is experienced over worthy causes; we speak of unholy *joy* over an enemy's downfall, but not of unholy *gladness*. *Delight* is a high degree of *pleasure*, often bubbling and rapturous. *Felicity*, a word in rather elevated use, is intense *happiness*. *Bliss* is perfect *joy*. *Contentment* is a state of calm *pleasure* over what one has or is; *satisfaction* leaves nothing to be desired. (413)

Writing an essay on Aristotelian "happiness," you must become sensitive to the differences between one word and another, even if you often use such terms synonymously. A dictionary with such mini-essays on refined usage will certainly help, and the best writers are always philologists, quietly and affectionately exploring the endless, and endlessly marvelous, territory of Dictionary Land. If you must use a thesaurus, always use it with a dictionary. I would make three other suggestions for improving your diction over time. First, study Latin, a language whose roots constitute a surprisingly large percentage of our language's words. Second, read widely. Third, imitate professors, especially the more articulate ones, by paying attention to their diction and remarking upon it as you listen, later trying it out. Refined diction may seldom be the possession of the young. How, though, do you think others acquired such a possession?

[4.5]   The study of diction begins with an elementary understanding of the parts of speech and their metaphysical implications, and it ends with an advanced practice of tactful, vital precision. There are nine parts of speech: the noun, the verb, the adjective, the adverb, the pronoun, the preposition, the conjunction, the verbal, and the interjection. It's worth reviewing them. First, as Weaver explains in his rhetoric, a noun is "a word which stands for a thing," but it is important to remember that a thing may be "an entity which is conceptual as well as one which is tangible" (305-06). In the following sentence, the nouns are both tangible and conceptual: "*Achilleus* could not control his *anger*." Second, a "verb is a word which asserts that something occurs or exists" (307). "Achilleus *watched* the battle": the verb indicates what its subject does or is. There are five further features of the verb that must be understood by the rhetor: tense, aspect, mood, voice, person, and number. A verb's tense indicates when it occurred; its aspect, the nature of the occurrence; its mood, the attitude of the agent of the occurrence; its voice, the passivity or activity of its subject. "Achilleus *watched* the battle." Tense of verb? Past. Aspect? Completed. Mood? Indicative. Voice? Active. Person? Third-person. Number? Singular. Third and fourth, an adjective "qualifies or limits the meaning of a noun" (310), and an adverb qualifies "the meaning of a verb, an adjective, or another adverb" (311): "*Swift-footed* Achilleus cried *desperately*." Fifth, a pronoun is a substitute for a noun: "Achilleus chased Hektor

around the city's walls, yet *he* could not catch *him*."
Sixth and seventh, preposition and conjunctions are
connection-words: "He chased them *into* the city *after* he came across the plain." Eighth, the verbal is a
word that, though fashioned from a verb, operates
as another part of speech. There are three: the infinitive, the participle, and the gerund. An infinitive is an infinite verb, without tense, aspect, mood,
voice, person, or number, that can be used as a noun,
adjective, or adverb: "*To love* Helen was Paris's one
achievement; she was the woman *to possess*; he desired *to be* with her." A participle is a verbal adjective: "*Appearing* before the Trojan elders, Helen
stunned them with her beauty." And the gerund is a
verbal noun: "*Possessing* Helen was the desire of both
Greek and Trojan." Ninth and last is the interjection, the part of speech dedicated to overwhelming
response. In *The Deluxe Transitive Vampire*, Karen
Elizabeth Gordon explains it well:

> An interjection is a word or a collection of
> words that express feeling. An outcast, set
> apart from the other seven parts of speech [she
> doesn't include the verbal as a part of speech],
> the interjection has little grammatical connection with its neighboring words or sentences.
> However, since it is strong, or emphatic, it
> doesn't really care. (28)

"*Oh!* When will this war ever end?": the interjection
of response. Every word is one of these parts of

speech—the noun, the verb, the adjective, the adverb, the pronoun, the preposition, the conjunction, the verbal, or the interjection—and many words can perform as more than one part of speech. In the metaphysics of grammar, each part of speech concerns one of three conditions—being, becoming, or relation: Nouns, pronouns, and adjectives concern being, and so too do both gerunds and participles, the first a verbal noun, the second a verbal adjective; verbs, infinitives (perhaps), and adverbs concern becoming; and prepositions and conjunctions concern relation. (The verb "to be" complicates this, of course, since, though a verb, it can concern a "state of being," and the interjection, in this as in so many things, simply doesn't fit.) Simply put, at the most fundamental level, a word will express what a thing is, what it does, or what its relationship to other things is. In *The Ethics of Rhetoric*, Weaver is quite convincing that the two most important parts of speech are the noun and the verb:

> The verb is regularly ranked with the noun in force, and it seems that these two parts of speech express the two aspects under which we habitually see phenomena, that of determining things and that of actions and states of being. Between them the two divide up the world at a pretty fundamental depth; and it is a commonplace of rhetorical instruction that a style made up predominantly of nouns and verbs will be a vigorous style. These are the symbols of the prime entities, words of stasis

> and words of movement . . . , which set forth
> the broad circumstances of any subject of dis-
> cussion. This truth is supported by the facts
> that the substantive is the heart of the gram-
> matical subject and the verb of a grammati-
> cal predicate. (135)

A rhetor who attends to nouns and verbs will be a better leader of souls toward any subject at hand because grammar discloses something constitutive of the world itself: everything has being, motion, and/or relation. Rhetoric is a liberal art because it concerns not only grammar, but also the nature of the world such grammar represents and enacts.

[4.6] The best diction is appropriate, precise, concise, and vivid. First, appropriateness is determined by your audience *[1.5]*. Academic audiences appreciate a more elevated diction than normal audiences, so, although you will not want to brandish a Johnsonian grandiloquence, you will need to employ a refined vocabulary. An academic audience, for example, will probably enjoy it if you characterize Odysseus's habitual caution as "prudence" or "circumspection"; in fact, your professor may have characterized it so during class. One of the signs of good student writing is that it employs with ease the vocabulary the course itself provides; such writing reveals not mere imitation, but complete understanding. If you characterize Odysseus as a "sneak," your reader may believe not only that your diction is not elevated enough, but also that your reflections are not being refined by the course itself. It ought to go without saying, of course, that one does not use vulgarities in academic writing. "Achilleus sucks": There may be an adolescent thrill in including this in an academic essay, but it will hardly be persuasive. It is the sort of comment that may very well be influential in an informal conversation with a peer, but it is hardly appropriate in written work for a university professor. The damage it will do to your *ethos* is difficult to measure. Second, diction should be not only appropriate, but also precise. The good rhetor knows how to discriminate between and among the slightly but significantly different meanings of words often used synonymously. Is Achilles merely "peeved" during Book I of the *Iliad*? Certainly not. Is he only "angry"? Not quite. He is "enraged": his anger is "the mania of intense indignation which only the unjustly dishonored experience." ("Mania," by the way, has as its root the Greek term *mênis* that Homer uses to name not only anger, but also *this form* of anger.) Precise diction persuades a reader that the rhetor is in command of the subject under discussion through his or her ability to discover, select, and employ a term that is *exact* enough to complete the argumentative work at hand. Third, appropriate, precise diction is necessary, but not sufficient. Many an otherwise good student sentence is undone by wordiness. Wordiness is a vice committed against economy, the virtue in rhetoric that achieves the greatest end with the fewest means. If it takes you thirty words to say what can be said in fifteen, you have wasted your reader's time. The following sentence is particularly wordy because the writer has repeated him or herself and has not cut away what the authors of *Prose Style* call "dead wood," or "superfluous wording" that can be deleted to improve a sentence's health (53):

> As a result of the fact that Achilleus is upset and angry with Agamemnon, he does not deliberate carefully and reflectively enough during the time in which the Assembly takes place.

This sentence both repeats and inflates itself: "As a result of the fact that" means "because"; to be "angry" is to be "upset"; "deliberation" assumes both "care" and "reflection"; "during the time when" means "while" or "during." A revised, more concise version of the above sentence might read thus: "Because Achilles is angry with Agamemnon, he does not deliberate during the Assembly." A sentence with thirteen words now does the work of one with thirty-one. One might argue that we have cut too much away, that one, for example, might debate without care or reflection. If that were so, we might revise accordingly: "Because Achilleus is angry with Agamemnon, he does not deliberate carefully and reflectively enough during the Assembly." This sentence still certainly exhibits greater economy than its original. The fourth and last characteristic of fine diction is vitality. When a rhetor uses words well, he or she actualizes their potential, releasing linguistic energy. There are any number of ways to ensure vitality in your prose, but the easiest is this: having chosen precise subjects, select vital verbs to refine any addiction you may have to the verb "to be." Do not say, "Achilleus is not concerned with his men"; say instead, "Achilleus *neglects* his men." Do not say, "Agamemnon's imprudence is responsible for the disaster of Hektor's rampage"; say instead, "Agamemnon's imprudence *releases* Hektor's rampage." If the verb is vivid enough, the rhetor is practicing personification. Agamemnon's imprudence is here treated as if it were a human being "releasing" Hektor's rampage. As this example testifies, vital diction will often be metaphoric, and the capacity to exploit the metaphoric capacities of one's language is perhaps the highest rhetorical power there is. We will examine metaphor later *[4.13–15]*. The best diction, then, is always appropriate, precise, concise, and vivid.

[4.7]   The rhetor is not only a lover of words but also a lover of phrases, clauses, and sentences, combinations of words. A phrase, according to Weaver in his rhetoric, is "a group of words which serves as a single part of speech and does not have a subject or a predicate" (319): "He chased all but Hektor *into the city*." A clause has at least one subject and one predicate—"*Achilleus rages*"—and comes in two forms, dependent and independent, which we will examine later *[4.8–10]*. A sentence too has at least one subject and one predicate: "The subject is the part [of a clause or sentence] about which the predicate makes an assertion; the predicate is the part which does the asserting" (322). If diction concerns the office of naming, a period concerns the office of assertion. The rhetor is a lover, then, of both naming and predicating. A good style's sentences will be varied in length and pattern, and they will be punctuated correctly. One cannot punctuate sentences properly, of course, without a knowledge of the four sentence types: the simple, the compound, the complex, and the compound-complex. A simple sentence (1) has one predication: "Hektor is a hero." A compound sentence (2) coordinates more than one predication: "Hektor is a hero, but Achilleus is not." A complex sentence (3) subordinates one predication to another: "Because Hektor is a hero, Achilleus cannot be one." A compound-complex sentence (4) combines (2) and (3): "Because Hektor serves the common good and Achilleus does not, Hektor is a hero and Achilleus is not." Rhetors will occasionally use short simple sentences and long compound-complex ones to vary their style, and they must often choose between the two defining patterns or styles, the coordinating and the subordinating.

[4.8]   The coordinating style depends heavily upon the coordination of independent clauses either by means of the comma and the coordinating conjunction or by means of the semi-colon. An independent clause (IC) has both a subject and a verb, and it may stand alone or it may be joined to another IC in one of two ways—either with a comma (,) and a coordinating conjunction (cc) or with a semi-colon (;). There are seven coordinating conjunctions: *and, but, or, for, nor, yet, so*. If the IC's are relatively long, then you must place a comma before the cc:

> Hektor is fighting on behalf of his family and his city, SO both his family and his city honor him for his devotion.

IC's may also be joined with only a semi-colon if they are very closely related in meaning:

> Hektor is fighting on behalf of his family and his city; both his family and his city honor him for his devotion.

Conjunctive adverbs (ca) do not alter the *IC; IC* pattern:

> Hektor is fighting on behalf of his family and his city; AS A CONSEQUENCE, both his family and city honor him for his devotion.

The conjunctive adverb is an excellent way to make transitions between clauses, periods, and paragraphs. Here are the most common: *accordingly, again, also, anyhow, besides, consequently, finally, furthermore, hence, however, indeed, likewise, moreover, otherwise, nevertheless, nonetheless, similarly, still, then, therefore.* Though the conjunctive adverb can indicate subtle relationships, it is nonetheless within the coordinating style. *IC, cc IC* and *IC; IC* and *IC; ca, IC*: all three are forms of coordination. The coordinating style is the style of The King James Version of the Bible, whose influence on English prose style is hard to overestimate, so I take an illustration from *Ecclesiastes*:

> I made me great works; I builded me houses; I planted me vineyards. I made me gardens and orchards, and I planted trees in them of all kinds of fruits. I made me pools of water to water therewith the wood that bringeth forth trees. I got me servants and maidens, and had servants born in my house; also, I had great possessions of great and small cattle above all that were in Jerusalem before me. I gathered me also silver and gold, and the peculiar treasure of kings and of provinces; I gat me men singers and women singers, and the delights of the sons of men, as musical instruments, and that of all sorts. So I was great, and increased more than all that were before me in Jerusalem; also, my wisdom remained with me. And whatsoever mine eyes desired I kept

not from them, I withheld not my heart from
any joy, for my heart rejoiced in all my labor,
and this was my portion of all my labor. Then
I looked on all the works that my hands had
wrought, and on the labor that I had labored
to do, and, behold, all was vanity and vexation of spirit, and there was no profit under
the sun. (2:4-11)

This is beautiful prose whose distinctive power is
the power of disposing equal phrases, clauses, and
sentences, coordinating them into a harmony which
itself appears to be an anatomy of the world. By bal-
ancing and juxtaposing, the coordinating style
achieves what Weaver calls in *The Ethics of Rhetoric*
"an equilibrium of forces" (124): "[T]he balanced
compound sentence, by the very contrivedness of
its structure, suggests something formed above the
welter of experience, and this form . . . transfers
something of itself to the meaning" (126). Coordination arranges the world into a balanced plenitude.
Imagine all the many delights discovered to be mere
vanity and vexation of the spirit!

[4.9] Though the subordinating style comes in
many forms, we will examine for now just one of its
forms, the joining of a dependent clause (DC) to an
IC. The DC becomes dependent because it begins
with a subordinating conjunction (sc), the most
common of which are the following: *after, although,*

as, because, before, how, if, since, though, unless, until, when, where, whereas, whether, and *while.* (One can always distinguish subordinate conjunctions from conjunctive adverbs by asking a simple question: Can the word move in its clause? If so, it's a conjunctive adverb. For example, one can write the following sentence either way: "Agamemnon is imprudent; however, Odysseus is prudent"; or, "Agamemnon is imprudent; Odysseus, however, is prudent." To move subordinate conjunctions around leads to gibberish. Try it.) Subordinate conjunctions can usually be classified into four types—temporal, causal, contingent, and concessive—and the classifications indicate what the relationship is between the DC and IC:

Temporal:	*After* Hektor made a poor decision, Troy fell.
Causal:	*Because* Achilleus left, the Greeks suffered.
Contingent:	*If* Odysseus had not disguised himself, the Suitors would have destroyed him.
Concessive:	*Though* Odysseus stayed with Kalypso for seven years, he was still faithful to Penelope.

The punctuation rule for such subordination is twofold: When the DC comes *before* the IC, it must be set off with a comma (***DC, IC***); it is usually not set off when the DC comes *after* the IC (***IC DC***). This last rule is qualified by the question of restriction: Does the DC restrict or limit the meaning of the IC? If so, then there is no comma; if not, there is. To illustrate the point, let me ask you to distinguish the following two sentences:

> (1) She didn't leave the party, *because she was intoxicated.*
>
> (2) She didn't leave the party *because she was intoxicated.*

What is the difference in meaning? In (1), she did not, in fact, leave the party, and the reason was her intoxication; in (2), however, she *did* leave the party, but did so, not because of intoxication, but because of some other reason, boredom perhaps. The DC in (1) is non-restrictive, so the comma is required; the DC in (2) is restrictive, so no comma is allowed. The restrictive/non-restrictive rule applies to relative clauses (RC) as well. An RC is a clause that begins with a relative pronoun—*who, which,* or *that.* You are now in a position to distinguish the two sentences below:

> (1) She left her boyfriend, who lives in San Francisco.
>
> (2) She left her boyfriend who lives in San Francisco.

Regardless of punctuation, subordination allows for greater possibilities of meaning than coordination.

Where the coordinating style balances equal parts, the subordinating style prioritizes unequal ones. Subordination represents greater complexity; as a consequence, it is the style of the sophisticated. If your style relies too often upon coordination, vary it by employing subordination, not only the dependent clause, but also the participial phrase—"*Thinking himself immune from human suffering*, Achilleus becomes pitiless"—or the medial or terminal appositive—"Patrokles, *Achilleus's one friend*, persuades him to allow him to enter the battle for one reason alone: *continued pride*"—or the relative clause—"Achilleus would not be persuaded by the one man *whom he despised above all others*, Odysseus." Perhaps the greatest practitioner of the subordinating style is Henry James, as you see in the compound-complex sentence from "The Art of Fiction": "It goes without saying that you will not write a good novel *unless you possess the sense of reality*, but it will be difficult to give you a recipe for calling that sense into being" (351). Though it is only partly captured here, James had a fine capacity to *sub*ordinate perceptions exactly, here for example the exact relationship between one's reality principle and one's novelistic powers: *Unless* one understands the real, one will not be able to write a novel.

[4.10] One of social reality's finest observers was Jane Austen, so it is no surprise to discover that she is a master of the compound-complex sentence; her sentences often provide both ampleness and discrimination, as we see here in Austen's representation of Elizabeth's response to Darcy's letter of proposal in *Pride and Prejudice*, one of the finer moments of this extraordinary novel:

> If Elizabeth, when Mr. Darcy gave her the letter, did not expect it to contain a renewal of his offers, she had formed no expectation at all of its contents. But such as they were, it may well be supposed how eagerly she went through them, and what a contrariety of emotion they excited. Her feelings as she read were scarcely to be defined. With amazement did she first understand that he believed any apology to be in his power; and steadfastly was she persuaded that he could have no explanation to give, which a just sense of shame would not conceal. With a strong prejudice against everything he might say, she began his account. . . . She read, with an eagerness which hardly left her power of comprehension, and from impatience of knowing what the next sentence might bring, was incapable of attending to the sense of the one before her eyes. (181)

Austen can be just to Elizabeth's excited and confused response only through subordination. As Weaver puts it in *The Ethics of Rhetoric*, subordination has a different power than coordination: "[T]he complex sentence does not appear until experience has undergone some refinement of the mind"; "because it goes beyond simple observation and begins to perceive things like causal principle, or begins to grade things according to a standard of interest, it brings in the notion of dependence to supplement that of simple togetherness" (121). A good rhetor, one of Austen's power, must undergo just such a refinement of mind, and his or her sentences must disclose such a mind not only by coordinating predications, but also by subordinating them within the subtle relationships of time, cause, contingency, and concession.

[4.11] Remember: If nouns represent what things are and verbs what they do, conjunctions—both those that coordinate and those that subordinate—represent how things are related. An inventive, harmonic argument must be enacted by a sentence whose diction is appropriate, precise, concise, and vivid and whose own structure is both varied and refined. This chapter has provided only general advice concerning diction, but it has provided eight specific sentence patterns and their respective punctuation:

1. *IC.*
2. *IC. IC.*
3. *IC, cc IC.*
4. *IC; IC.*
5. *IC; ca, IC.*
6. *DC, IC*

7. *IC, DC (non-restrictive)*.
8. *IC DC (restrictive)*.

The first two patterns exemplify the simple sentence; the third through the fifth, the compound; and the sixth through the eighth, the complex. This list is hardly exhaustive, nor will it answer every one of your questions about syntax and punctuation, but, if you memorize these eight patterns, your style will improve enormously. If Weaver is right that sentences remake the world, if only a little, then only the balanced plenitude of coordination and the perceptive refinement of subordination will make it possible for a rhetor and his or her audience to see rich juxtapositions and fine relationships within abundant and subtle ideas, events, texts, and artifacts.

[4.12] Within both coordination and subordination, there is a rule which is also a resource for writing correct and long sentences: the rule of parallelism. Words, phrases, and clauses that are equal in function must be equal in form. The following sentence is unparallel: "Achilleus listens to the ambassadors' arguments, responds to each, and is ignoring all." The three verbs—"listens," "responds," and "ignores"—must be in the same form. The rule is a resource too, though. Whenever possible, multiply parallel words, phrases, and clauses to fashion longer, more interesting sentences. Below is the first sentence of The Declaration of Independence, a sentence that has forward momentum because of parallel structure and only can compel a reader's interest because the parallel structure is varied before it becomes tedious. I have tried to visualize its profoundly persuasive parallelism:

We hold these truths to be self-evident:
> ***that*** all men *are created* equal;
> ***that*** they *are endowed* by their creator with <u>inherent</u> and <u>inalienable</u> rights;
> ***that*** among these are <u>life,</u> <u>liberty</u> and <u>the pursuit of happiness;</u>
> ***that*** to secure these rights, governments *are instituted* among men,
>> DERIVING their just powers from the consent of the governed;
>
> ***that*** whenever any form of government becomes destructive of these ends, it is the right of the people <u>to alter</u> or <u>abolish</u> it and <u>to institute</u> new government,
>> LAYING its foundation *on such principles*, and
>> ORGANIZING its powers *in such form*, as to them shall seem most likely to effect their <u>safety</u> and <u>happiness.</u>

We see in this one sentence all the virtues of style so far discussed. More specifically, Jefferson puts into parallel structure his words, phrases, and clauses, and he varies the structure once established; such varied parallelism allows him to include a great deal more invented, organized points than would be possible without its deep structure, a structure a reader experiences even if he or she is not fully aware of it. It could be said that our country was invented with a fine sentence.

[4.13] Parallelism is actually a "figure of speech," a sentence pattern that varies the ordinary or conventional use of language. Figures come in two types, those which vary standard word order and those which vary standard word usage: a figure is either a scheme or a trope. If parallelism is the most important scheme, metaphor is the most important trope. Metaphor is like simile since both compare two items; a metaphor is an identity, however, where a simile is an analogy. A metaphor says, "X is Y"; a simile says, "X is like Y." Even so, the figure of metaphor encompasses simile. Both draw out resemblances between things not immediately akin to one another, and, when the reader discovers the resemblance, he or she is pleased. (Aristotle even suggests in the *Rhetoric* that metaphors are like riddles.) In the passage below from Samuel Johnson's "Preface to Shakespeare"—still the single best piece of Shakespeare criticism there is—one sees Johnson employing metaphor to explain Shakespeare's figure of the pun—a verbal vice, according to Johnson, one he calls the "quibble":

A quibble is to Shakespeare, what luminous vapors are to the traveler; he follows it at all adventures, it is sure to lead him out of his way, and sure to engulf him in the mire. It has some malignant power over his mind, and its fascinations are irresistible. Whatever be the dignity of profundity of his disquisition, whether he be enlarging knowledge or exhalting affection, whether he be amusing attention with incidents, or enchaining it in suspense, let but a quibble spring up before him, and he leaves his work unfinished. A quibble is the golden apple for which he will always turn aside from his career, or stoop from his elevation. A quibble, poor and bar-ren as it is, gave him such delight, that he was content to purchase it, by the sacrifice of rea-son, propriety and truth. A quibble was to him the fatal Cleopatra for which he lost the world, and was content to lose it. (273-74)

This is magnificently metaphoric prose. Its force is the result of three extended similes, each one of which can be given the SAT structure of "as-A-is-to-B-so-C-is-to-D": A:B::C:D. Here are all three:

1) quibble:Shakespeare::vapors:traveler
2) quibble:Shakespeare::golden apple:Atalanta
3) quibble:Shakespeare::Cleopatra:Antony

All three are rhetorically brilliant. The first is self-explanatory, but the second and third are allusions. The second requires that you remember classical myth, in particular the story of Atalanta and Hippomenes. Atalanta was a woman who did not want to marry and also happened to be an especially fast runner. Her father set up races between Atalanta and her suitors. If one of them won, he would get to marry her; if not, he was executed. Hippomenes tricked her in his race by dropping golden apples in her way, apples that distracted her from her race, and beat his new bride. Johnson argues that "puns" were golden apples distracting Shakespeare from his true course. The third requires remembering that Antony lost both the Roman empire and his life for the love of Cleopatra. All three metaphors suggest that "puns" destroyed Shakespeare's pursuit of reason, propriety, and truth. The humor here is the result of its metaphoric richness, during which the rhetor re-imagines one thing in terms of another.

[4.14] Two of the most important points to remember about metaphoric language, as a writer, are to refrain from repeating banal or clichéd metaphors, those which have lost their metaphoric energy, and to avoid mixing metaphors. Many metaphors have been repeated so often that they no longer appear to be metaphors. They are "dead metaphors," or clichés. Little rhetorical energy attaches to the saying that Agamemnon is "as slow as an ox"; there's quite a bit more in saying he's "as slow as a chariot that has lost both its wheels." Dead metaphors often get mixed since the writer doesn't know that they are metaphors and, consequently, doesn't realize that two metaphoric fields can't be harvested at once. Accidentally combining clichés leads to howlers. The authors of *Prose Style* have discovered a particularly awful one: "One notorious example [of mixed metaphor] originated with an American radio announcer who, after informing his listeners that World War II was over, declared joyously that 'the Fascist octopus has finally sung his swan song'" (182). Of course, if the announcer had avoided both clichés, he wouldn't have mixed them up. Metaphor is a matter of imagining new relationships between entities often sundered in the conventional comprehension of things. Thus, repeating dead metaphors misses the point, and mixing dead metaphors confuses it. I should point out two cautions about metaphor. First, this metaphoric capacity is very difficult to learn. One way to strengthen that capacity, though, is to read poetry, a form of rhetoric whose central figure of speech is metaphor. Second, readers can handle only so many metaphors in prose. Students who experiment with metaphoric language will often end up, at first anyway, with "purple prose," prose so dense with metaphors that the reader gets tangled in the dense web of figuration. Reimagine the world through metaphoric language, then use it sparingly.

[4.15] That re-imagining may be the highest exercise of the rhetorical faculty, since important metaphors, those metaphors which we forget are metaphors, become ways of structuring our understanding of the world. When a student says, "I see what you mean," he or she may not realize that a metaphor is being employed—intellectual understanding is physical sight—yet it is there nonetheless. Some metaphors are so common that they become concepts. Indeed, George Lakoff and Mark Johnson, the authors of *Metaphors We Live By,* argue, and conclusively prove, that "human thought processes are largely metaphorical" (6). "Metaphor" literally means "carrying across," the transference of meaning from one field to another. What Lakoff and Johnson prove is as true of our concepts as it is of our metaphors because they turn out to be the same activity. Remember that the offices of rhetoric—invention, organization, and style—are inseparable, even if you can distinguish them for learning's sake. The last resource of style, metaphor, turns out to be the first resource of invention, and the writer needs to become aware of that human fact in order to have at his or her command the central resource of culture itself, our metaphoric grasp of the world.

[4.16] Mr. Heyne's essay is full of fine words and sentences. Re-read his essay *[Appendix* 1*]*, reflecting on its style. It's worth examining one sentence in detail:

> Still requiring divine motivation, Telemachos receives a dream from Athene in which she gives him a plan to return to Ithaka and avoid the ambush of the suitors. (3)

The diction here is appropriate, precise, concise, and vivid. The nouns are lucid— "dream," "plan" and "ambush"—and the verbs energetically antithetical— "receives" and "gives." He varies his style with an opening participial phrase—"Still requiring divine motivation"—which functions as a verbal adjective describing the subject of the IC: "Telemachos receives a dream from Athena." And the subordination of the RC—"in which she gives him a plan to return to Ithaka"—lets him discuss the fact of the dream and its content, all the while subordinating its content to its occurrence, which is appropriate given that he wants to stress the "divine" motivation still required. The parallelism of the infinitive phrases—"to plan" and "[to] avoid"—lays out a sequence common to the dream and the story's future narrative. Throughout the sentence and the essay, the reader knows that he or she is in the hands of a mature stylist.

[4.17] A writer's style is composed of his or her diction and periods, both of which must be parallel, varied, and correct to be persuasive. Even this is not enough, however. Academic work must also be professional to be persuasive, edited until it is letter-perfect, formatted correctly, and printed clearly and darkly on decent paper. Such last-minute matters often annoy students, primarily because they leave such matters until the very last moment, if not later. But a fine essay—inventive, orderly, and styled—that is nonetheless sloppy will not exhibit the requisite care of words and things called for by the importance of the rhetorical situation, the leading of your reader's soul toward the reality of the subject by means of language, a rhetorical situation that will be evaluated by an academic audience, your professor. Although a good grade is not an end in itself, it is one of your goals nonetheless, so it is worth attending to every detail. Care exhibited with respect to *all* compositional matters: this is the sign of the highest persuasiveness in the art of rhetoric.

5

Re-Vision:

Products and Processes

[5.1] Throughout our discussion of invention, organization, and style, we have discussed the aspects of writing as though they were attributes of the written product, and they certainly are that, yet they are also the result of a process. Now writing processes are notoriously idiosyncratic: Everyone has his or her own way of writing; that "way" may very well be an object of great attachment. Some people, for example, cannot stand to write without a detailed outline to follow; others love to write without one. I once found it painful to write a sentence that had *any* errors in it, but I got over it and learned that ignoring some things allowed me to concentrate more fully on others. Even though writing processes are idiosyncratic, I describe here a single one which I believe students can alter to suit their own methods. In short, I suggest isolating each of the canons of rhetoric—invention, organization, and style—as one stage in the process of writing a paper, segregating each to perfect it. First, invent a thesis and the proofs to defend it; second, organize that invented material into either the Immanent Design or the Classical Oration form; third, revise your diction and periods for clarity, correctness, and variety. Now I concede that such isolation is unnatural; after all, the three canons are not actually discrete. Even so, isolation works. Tennis players, for example, often practice their backhand during a workout, even though no one ever played a set of tennis using only his or her backhand. The player practices by isolating one particular skill in order to strengthen it for the time when, in relation to all his or her other skills, it's needed. So too with writers: isolating skills strengthens them. There are three parts to our discussion of the writing process: First, the three canons as stages in that process; second, the nature of revision based on commentary; and third, the particular challenge of the in-class essay, a form that will not allow one to isolate and revise.

[5.2]   As Peter Elbow explains in *Writing with Power*, one of the greatest dangers of novice writers is "trying to write it right the first time" (39):

> When the method works magically—that is, when you tap your deepest powers and cook everything completely before you write any-

thing down—sometimes there is a finer integration and connectedness than you can achieve by revising. And even when it works only adequately—that is, when you merely settle on something that happens to be on the surface of your mind and then write it out— you may be able to write your piece more quickly and with less uncertainty than if you used two steps.

But it is a dangerous method because it puts more pressure on you and depends for its success on everything's running smoothly. If you are out of practice or insecure or just a bit off your form, you can take longer trying to get something right the first time than you would have needed for writing roughly and then revising. Indeed, the method often fails outright. That is, you can sit there and think and stare into space, try to make an outline, perhaps try beer and naps and walks, and still not figure out what you want to say—or even *anything* to say. That need to get it right prevents the ingredients in your head from cooking, developing, progressing. (42)

Elbow's solution to the danger of "trying to write it right the first time" is revision. Re-vision, or "seeing again," is not the same as editing. When you edit, you clean up after all the major work is done; when you revise, you do the work itself. After you've read the prompt and reflected on your audience, subject, and purpose *[1.5]*, write a rough draft of the essay.

Do not be anxious about its quality; it's just a draft. Save and print it. (I assume throughout that you are writing on a computer.) You are now ready for an invention revision.

[5.3] Isolate the canon of invention and, reading your essay aloud to yourself, address the following questions about your draft:

> 1. Does the essay address the assignment?
>
> 2. Is the essay's focus sharp enough, given the assignment's expectations?
>
> 3. What is the thesis? Is it determinate and encompassing enough?
>
> 4. Are its ideas developed enough? Is its logic strong?
>
> 5. Is its textual explication full, and are its analysis and synthesis persuasive?

Each question will reveal areas of improvement. If the essay does not answer the assignment *[2.1]*, then revise it so it does. You may, for example, have avoided or misunderstood one of its questions; realizing this allows you to address it again. If your focus *[2.2]* isn't sharp enough—if, that is, you are using a map of your state to get from your dorm to a class—sharpen it. If you are trying to prove that Agamemnon is not a good leader in two to three pages, for example, narrow your focus to determine whether he fulfills *one*, instead of *three*, of the characteristics of a good leader. If you don't have a thesis *[2.3]*, invent one; if you have one, but it isn't determinate enough, articulate it further; if it doesn't encompass all your proofs, dilate it so that it does. If you have not developed your ideas *[2.4–14]*, do so. Strengthen your reasoning; define important terms. If you haven't explicated the text *[2.15]*, analyze an important piece of text *[2.16]* and synthesize the parts of the text into a sense of the whole *[2.17]*. (One of Mr. Heyne's earlier drafts was missing his proof that Telemachos is not only ready to help his father restore the kingdom, but also ready to rule on his own, an important argument since it augments our understanding both of the young man's maturation and of the kingdom's restoration: he must become self-sufficient, and a healthy regime prepares the young to become just that.) Having revised the essay's focus, thesis, development, and explication, you will have a new draft, one that will be, no doubt, a mess. Save and print it. You can order it during the next stage of revision.

[5.4] Forget invention and concentrate on organization. You may now dispose all of the newly invented material by addressing these five questions:

> 1. Is the introduction strong: Does it provide an outline of proofs and the thesis?
>
> 2. Is the body strong: Do the proofs cohere?
>
> 3. Is the conclusion strong?

111

4. Are the paragraphs unified and coherent?

5. Are the transitions between parts, paragraphs, and sentences strong?

One of the easiest ways to begin to understand the shape of your essay is this: Number its paragraphs; then, mark the division both between the introduction *[3.4–7]* and the body *[3.8–10]* and between the body and the conclusion *[3.11–13]*; within the body or proof, investigate the order of points to see if there is indeed a recognizable sequence. Once you have ascertained the sequence, write an internal outline of the sequenced proofs and revise the paragraphs and transitions accordingly *[3.14]*. If there are problems with the introduction or conclusion, try one of the techniques suggested in Chapter 3. (The last sentence of Mr. Heyne's concluding paragraph, for example, was, in an earlier draft, its first sentence; by moving it to the end, it provided him with framing sentences for the entire essay.) Once you've revised your organization, save and print.

[5.5]   Now forget invention and organization. Address, instead, your draft's style by answering these questions:

1. Is the diction appropriate, precise, concise, and vivid?

2. Is the grammar correct?

3. Is the punctuation correct?

112

4. Are the periods varied in length and pattern? Are there any strong metaphors?

5. Is the essay formatted by the appropriate standards?

Revising diction *[4.4–6]* requires that you attend to your words; varying sentence length and pattern requires that you combine sentences by means of coordination *[4.8]*, subordination *[4.9-10]* and/or parallelism *[4.12]*. Examine each sentence for grammar and punctuation *[4.5, 4.6-10]*. If you have particular problems here that you commonly make, then you should set aside some time to remedy those by working through the exercises in a handbook. (Mr. Heyne has a fine prose style, and it comes rather easily to him; even so, he spent a good deal of revision time on concision so that he could pack as much proof into his page-count as possible.) Imitate the student essay in ***Appendix*** I for format and see an appropriate handbook for any other style matters. Save and print. Edit the entire essay by reading this penultimate draft backwards, paragraph by paragraph, correcting anything you see. Change and save; print two copies of this last draft—one for the professor and one for you; finally, turn it in on time.

[5.6]   During this process, you will have missed a great deal that another reader—a professor, a tutor or a peer—might well have discerned; as a consequence, it is always a good idea "to get a reading" of your essay sometime during the writing process. Having completed a draft, I always have it reviewed by a colleague, and this book has had many readings to bring it to completion, including at least one from an editor whose job it is to help authors revise their written work. Such readings allow you to improve your writing by disclosing problems and potential solutions. Professors, tutors, and peers will read your written work and offer commentary in the margins to help strengthen the essay's invention, organization, and style. They are not writing the essay for you; rather, they are offering criticism that you will have to address. Peers too, either formally in class during peer-review workshops or informally outside of class in conversations, may offer such advice. To ensure focused response from peers, use the peer-review form provided *[Appendix 3]*. By revising your essay in response to this feedback, you will discover that your essay may change radically, that through commentary and revision it becomes what it potentially was all along. Actualizing the potential in all our writing, the artful increase of the persuasiveness of one's own work and one's friends' work, is *the* goal of a writing community. Mr. Heyne's essay, for example, could certainly be strengthened through revision. Even so, there comes a time when you must simply finish, not because the essay is perfect, but because, within the particular case, you have discovered all of the available means of persuasion you could. One can only lead from the point where one is, and that point changes with experience and education. A fine freshman essay will not be as good as a fine senior presentation; a fine senior presentation, not as good as a fine Master's thesis, and so on. We are all trying to improve our writing as we refine our understanding of the world about which we write.

[5.7]   This rhetorical understanding of discourse, the idea that we do as well as we can within the contingencies at hand, allows you to relax in otherwise stressful academic situations—the in-class essay, for example, a genre that calls for instant perfection. This genre is crucial to your academic career because in humanities classes it is the most common form of evaluating your class performance. Even a class without a paper—shame on any class in the humanities without at least one—will have examinations that call for in-class writing. Having prepared for an in-class essay, one should relax; after all, it is too late and anxiety will certainly not improve your game. There are four steps in this rhetorical situation: reading, outlining, writing, and editing. First, read carefully the directions and the prompt and understand what you are expected to do. Underline important directions and identify the parts of the prompt, reflecting as you do on what you believe your professor wants you to accomplish. Examine the following prompt:

When Demodocus sings his first song in *The Odyssey*, it concerns "the quarrel between Odysseus and . . . Achilleus" (8.75), a quarrel that has no other legendary source. Suppose Homer is speaking indirectly of his own two epic heroes, and suppose there is a tension in the two works between Achillean heroism and Odyssean. Compare/contrast Achilleus and Odysseus in both works in order to answer this question: What are their respective virtues, or excellences; how are those virtues alike, how different; and what does the difference reveal about Homer's conception of the heroic in the *Iliad* and the *Odyssey*?

Notice both that the prompt employs a topic of invention—comparison *[2.13]*—and that there are three main questions. The prompt is asking you both to synthesize Homer's two poems by focusing on their main characters and to answer the three questions. Such prompts are quite common. Second, begin, not with invention, but with organization; in this particular case, since you will not be able to revise, you should choose a shape at the beginning. Choose either the form of the Classical Oration or the form that is immanent within the prompt itself. Prompts often have within them a suggested arrangement. If there are two questions, for example, answer them in the order asked. Scribble an outline down for yourself. The preceding prompt might suggest the following outline, for example:

116

You might discover some other, more inventive shape within your own case, but you should begin with some provisional order. Third, as you write, attend to clarity and correctness in your sentences because you will not have time to revise. Fourth, watch your time very carefully so that you can complete the essay in the allotted time, leaving yourself a few minutes at the end to read and edit your essay once. As always, allow your own writing process to inform this advice. Indeed, allow yourself to forget such advice, as well; if all goes well, after all, you should lose yourself in the subject at hand and the pleasure that attends reflection upon it. You cannot lose yourself entirely, however, and such double-consciousness—aware of time during the exam, lost in timeless speculation about Homer—requires experience to master and enjoy.

[5.8]   If a writer procrastinates long enough, of course, then any essay resembles an in-class essay with respect to the required dispatch, so you may

117

have to employ the four-step method above for any last-minute essays. You will face an enormous amount of writing, so some of it will be hurried. Fortunately, leisure and care on some essays will improve the rhetorical power of all your essays. When you do have the time, employ it well to refine your writing process, because, although it is true that almost any process will allow you to survive, only a refined one—guided by the principles of the standards of evaluation and all the while critiqued, encouraged, and inspired by the rhetorical community of your university—will produce a soul-leading word that rises to the understanding of the world. That is the word you hope to discover and share. If you practice your art *as* an art, strengthening the process to perfect the product, you will produce such a word.

6

Conclusion: Rhetoric as the Office of Assertion

[6.1]   This conclusion can be brief. "The sentence through its office of assertion is a force adding itself to the forces of the world": Richard Weaver articulates the defining principle of the classical rhetorical tradition—rhetoric moves an audience, and that movement is a "force" because all agents of influence move others. This movement can take two forms. In the first form, one moves others without their awareness or consent. This motion can appear to be a kind of magic, the rhetor casting a spell on his or her audience, and, in fact, some theorists of rhetoric believe that is exactly what rhetoric essentially is. In the second form, though, one moves another to move him or herself. What is so compelling about rhetoric is that the true rhetorical spell does not corrupt, but rather restores and exercises the liberty of reflection and action on behalf of rhetor and audience. In the rhetorical community of a good university, rhetors become audiences, and audiences rhetors. This is another way of saying that, in such a Socratic environment, every teacher is a student and every student a teacher, both giver and receiver of slight but distinct attractions toward reality.

[6.2] It may seem strange to consider invention *[2]*, organization *[3]*, and style *[4]* as forms of attraction, but that is what they are. When you persuade readers to believe *[1.3–8]* that your thesis *[2.3]* is true because you have defended it with developed ideas *[2.4–14]* and explicated text *[2.15–17]*; because you have arranged that developed, explicit thesis into a cosmic whole *[3.1–2]* with a beginning *[3.3–7]*, a middle *[3.8–10]*, and an end *[3.11–13]*; because you have styled that harmonic case with mature diction *[4.4–6]*, artful predications *[4.7–11]*, and imaginative figures of speech *[4.12–15]*: When you persuade readers thus, you are attracting them toward a truer grasp of the idea, event, text, or artifact under discussion, moving them closer to it. The motive character of rhetoric explains Plato's understanding in the *Phaedrus* that rhetoric is the art of soul-leading through language, that rhetoric is essentially erotic, arousing as it does our desire to move toward the real that is manifest in any true word. A fine essay is a gift.

[6.3] One might go so far as to say that the office of assertion is *the* office of human association. In all

of your many offices, you are what Weaver calls in
The Ethics of Rhetoric a "language citizen":

> Like the political citizen defined by Aristotle,
> language citizenship makes one a potential
> magistrate, or one empowered to decide. The
> work is best carried on, however, by those who
> are aware that language must have some con-
> nection to the intelligential world, and that is
> why one must think about the rhetorical na-
> ture even of grammatical categories. (142)

The language citizenship you acquire during your
undergraduate career will certainly prepare you for
many other offices—in your personal, academic, and
professional lives—and in this regard your rhetorical education will certainly be practical. There is little
writing you will do from this point on that will not
be improved by attention to your class essays. Such
citizenship is not simply utilitarian, nor is it instruction that simply "norms" the young to serve society,
a sacrifice of self. In his discussion of bilingual education in *Hunger of Memory*, Richard Rodriguez dis-
tinguishes between private and public individuality
in order to celebrate the adulthood of what Weaver
calls "language citizenship":

> But the bilingualists simply scorn the value
> and necessity of assimilation. They do not re-
> alize that there are *two* ways a person is indi-
> vidualized. So they do not realize that while

> one suffers a diminished sense of *private* indi-
> viduality by becoming assimilated into pub-
> lic society, such assimilation makes possible
> the achievement of public individuality. (26)

Whether you agree with Rodriguez on bilingual education or not, his point stands: public individuality,
what the classical rhetoricians might call *ethos*, requires that you have command of the public language. Though not in the least romantic, the classical rhetorical tradition may very well be the best way
to cultivate your public individuality.

[6.4] This would, indeed, be a civic good, a good
that would, I believe, improve our democratic culture. The more articulate our citizens, the more productive and flourishing would be our economic and
civic life. Even so, such a rhetorical education is a
good in and of itself, a liberal art. What is the good
of understanding and employing language well during occasions of public individuality? In *A Room of
One's Own*, Virginia Woolf explains that the language
citizen or public individual—the writer—has a greater
share of reality: "Now the writer, as I think, has the
chance to live more fully than other people in the
presence of this reality. It is his business to find it
and collect it and communicate it to the rest of us"
(114). All liberal arts, in both the sciences and the
humanities, are animated by the fundamental human desire to know, the fulfillment of which is a

good, even if it provides no economic or political benefit whatsoever. An education for economic productivity and political utility *alone* is an education for slaves, but an education for finding, collecting, and communicating reality is an education for free people, people free to know what is so. Remember, knowing the real is a good before it is a power. What is that reality? Well, that, you see, is the very question *you* will need to answer as you take up the office of assertion, asserting where you stand, and standing afterwards in the presence of what you have asserted. Reader: stand by your word.

Appendix 1

Tommy Heyne
English 1301: Literary Tradition I
Dr. Scott Crider
November 22

The Maturation of Telemachos

1 Though Homer's *Odyssey* concentrates primarily on the homecoming of Odysseus and the restoration of his household and polity, the minor character Telemachos is still essential to the restoration of this household and kingdom. In many ways, a parallel can be drawn between the action of Telemachos in Homer's great epic and the action of Hamlet in Shakespeare's great tragedy. At the beginning of Shakespeare's play, Hamlet is in mourning for his father in a blithely feasting household in which an inferior man tries to replace his father, the old king. Only with a supernatural apparition and enlightening message does Hamlet begin to move towards manly action. Slowly throughout the play, by going on a voyage and by hearing about and observing characters such as Fortinbras and Laertes, who do act manfully in desiring revenge for their fathers, Hamlet is impelled towards bloody thoughts. Finally, Hamlet returns to his palace, receives further supernatural impetus, and cleanses his household of the evil man who tried to replace his father. *Hamlet* helps us see the function of the Ithakan prince in the *Odyssey*. Telemachos's maturation, through supernatural and human influence, into a man capable of acting as he ought to is essential to the restoration of the Odyssean household and regime because, once matured, Telemachos is able to help Odysseus forcibly get rid of the suitors, and also because Telemachos—unlike Hamlet—becomes a viable heir who will maintain the same high standards set by Laertes and Odysseus.

2 Telemachos's primary action in the *Odyssey* is in maturing from a child to a man, from one who is incapable of acting as he should to one who is capable. At the start of the epic, Telemachos is still a child; the only men who have been his role models for all of his twenty years are the boorish suitors and the distant swineherd. In order to catch up on the maturing that had been stalled for two decades, Telemachos needs special assistance and new role models. In fact, Telemachos is first moved towards manly action only through divine intervention. Athene comes to him, in the disguise of Mentes, as Telemachos sits "among the suitors, his heart deep grieving within him, / imagining in his mind his great father" (Homer 1.114–15). She tells him, "You should not go on / clinging to your childhood. You are no longer of an age to do that" (1.296–97). Athene gives him the role models of his father and Orestes, so that he can think of what they would do in a similar situation. She then tells Telemachos to call an assembly and sail for Pylos and Sparta to get news of his father. Athena leaves, "but she left in his spirit / determination and courage, and he remembered his father / even more than he had before" (1.320–22). When Telemachos does boldly announce to the suitors that he will call an assembly in which he will tell the suitors "forthright" to leave and will pray that they die if they continue to ruin his household, "all of them bit their lips, in amazement / at Telemachos and the daring way he had spoken to them" (1.374, 381–82). Each succeeding time in the epic that Telemachos speaks boldly to them, as the man of the house ought to, they show this same amazement, which demonstrates that they are used to seeing him act as a child but now see a new authority that signals growing maturity.

3 Yet, even with the first appearance of Athene, Telemachos is far from becoming a man; he still acts childishly and requires further assistance to mature. A glaring example is seen just moments after Athene leaves him and Penelope comes down to request that Phemios sing a different song. Telemachos immaturely tells his mother off, saying, "Go therefore back in the house, and take up your own work. . . . For mine is the power in this household" (1.356, 359).

Though Telemachos treats the haughty suitors as he ought, he does not treat his mother well. This shows that maturing, even when accelerated, is a slow learning process. Telemachos still requires assistance to call the assembly: "Athene drift[s] an enchantment of grace upon" Telemachos, and Aigyptios gives him a good omen (2.12). He also requires Athene's help to round up a crew, sail for Pylos, and gather up the "courage" necessary to speak to Nestor (3.76). Nestor again presents Orestes, the boy who became a man by avenging his father, as a model for Telemachos. More concretely, Nestor also gives his son Peisistratos to Telemachos to guide him, both literally (to Sparta) and figuratively (to manhood). In fact, when Telemachos observes how Peisistratos speaks to Menelaos, Telemachos is able to speak to him as well, to ask the whereabouts of his father. Telemachos, actualizing his genetic disposition to tactfulness, speaks so wisely that Menelaos says, "You are of true blood, dear child, in the way you reason" (4.611). Still requiring divine motivation, Telemachos receives a dream from Athene in which she gives him a plan to return to Ithaka and avoid the ambush of the suitors. Yet, much as with the first divine appearance episode, Telemachos becomes so intent on accomplishing this plan, as he ought to do, that he forgets to do another thing that he ought to do. Only with the urging of Peisistratos does he realize that he should stay at Sparta at least long enough to receive grand "gifts of friendship" from Menelaos and Helen

(15.55). After receiving these gifts and parting from Peisistratos, the mini-odyssey of Telemachos is nearly complete, and Telemachos begins to act as a man without any immediate influence prompting him to do so. The prophetic Theoklymenos comes to Telemachos, supplicates him, and asks for sanctuary, and Telemachos agrees. This proper treatment of another, a suppliant in this case, is a portent of the new Telemachos, who is able to use the instruction and models he has received to act as a man should.

4 After his odyssey, Telemachos generally acts as a man, though he is still learning. He treats the beggar, who—unbeknownst to him—is his father, kindly by saying, "No, sit my friend, and we shall find another seat" when Odysseus begins to get up to yield his seat to his son (16.43). Yet he is still somewhat insolent to his mother, who greets him in tears, saying to him, "[T]ell me what sights you have been seeing" (17.44). Instead of sympathizing with his poor, worrying mother and granting her simple request, he replies to her, "Mother, do not stir up a scene of sorrow, nor trouble / my heart once more" (17.46–47). Later, Penelope indirectly says how Telemachos's impatience, indifference, and impertinence have made her sorrowful (17.101–06). Even so, learning from his mother, he does respect her request and does relate the story of his travels. After the beggar Odysseus enters the household and Telemachos boldly defends him from the haughty suitors, Penelope comes down and scolds

Telemachos in hopes of further helping her son mature. Though her criticism is even more direct and less true this time, Telemachos does not tell his mother off as he did before. Instead, he says, "My mother, I cannot complain of your anger" (18.227). Telemachos has gone far enough along his road to maturation that he is able to treat his mother as she should be treated even though he does not have a god or helpful friend directly telling him to do so.

5 Telemachos is so much more obliging here because he knows that his father is in the same room, and it is this concrete fatherly influence that helps him come to complete maturity at last. He observes and learns from his father's cleverness and his self-control, and tries to imitate him. Also, he knows that his father is watching him and that it is his duty to maintain the household and protect Odysseus until Odysseus becomes ruler of it again. Telemachos steps up to the challenge and so shows himself ready, or almost ready, to govern Ithaka should Odysseus die. After Eurymachos throws a stool at Odysseus and "the suitors were raising a tumult," Telemachos diffuses the potentially dangerous situation by tactfully asking that they go home (18.399). After Ktesippos throws an ox hoof at Odysseus, Telemachos shows the extent of his maturity by saying, "[If you had hit the beggar] I would have struck you with my sharp spear fair in the middle. . . . Let none display any rudeness / here in my house. I now notice all and know of it, better / and worse alike, but before I was only an infant" (20.306, 308–10).

Telemachos now notices injustice in the kingdom and knows it for what it is. Afterwards, he amazes all with his maturity and control of the situation: he announces the contest, sets up the axes, tells Eumaios very forcibly to give the bow to Odysseus, takes his fighting place next to Odysseus, helps accomplish Odysseus's plan to slaughter the suitors, and even speaks up to his father to save the herald and the singer. Yet, as Eurykleia points out, Telemachos is but "lately come of age," and he still cannot yet completely match up to the man that his father is (22.426). This is represented in his lack of complete physical maturity, since he has much more trouble with stringing the bow than Odysseus does. It is also represented in his nearly fatal, though completely accidental, error of leaving the store room open. Yet Telemachos admits his error, saying, "Father, it is my mistake" (22.325). Telemachos's last spoken lines show that there is great hope for the line of Laertes and Odysseus, and that—with the assistance of Athene, Nestor, Peisistratos, Penelope, Odysseus, and others—he has finally reached manly maturity; though he may make an accidental, immature mistake, he is capable of acting as he ought. He says, "As far as my will goes / I will not shame the blood that comes from you" (24.511-12).

6 Observing Telemachos's essential action of maturation, one begins to realize its importance to the greater, central action of the work—the restoration of Odysseus's household and polity. In fact, Telemachos's maturity is essential to this restoration. An important reason for this is that Telemachos, because he has become a man, is able to help his father slay the suitors. Before Telemachos becomes mature, he is courageous only when inspired by another, such as Athene. Hence, at the start of the epic, Telemachos is hardly fit to throw insults, much less spears, at the suitors. He first earns social, rhetorical courage as he is inspired to directly address the suitors, Nestor, and Menelaos. He later is able to learn martial courage, as he realizes just how violent the suitors' intentions are and as he uses Orestes and his father as models to inspire him to warlike behavior. Telemachos hears from Athene of the suitors' "longing to kill" him, and, realizing the gravity of the situation, plots the slaughter of the suitors with his father (15.30). The plotting is not completely one-sided; Odysseus needs his son to speak of "the number of suitors" and any possible allies (16.235). More and more Telemachos demonstrates his ability to aid his father in the deadly plans. As described before, once back in the palace, Telemachos succeeds in defending his father "against the blows and the insults / of all the suitors" (20.263–64). Alone, friendless, and unarmed, Odysseus would stand little chance against all of the suitors, should they all raise a "tumult" against him (18.399). Telemachos also aids Odysseus in accomplishing his plan. "His heart full of guile," Telemachos removes some of the arms, seats Odysseus in the hall, and has Eurykleia lock the doors (20.257). Once the bloody "feasting" begins, Telemachos takes a large share in the general slaughter, killing Amphimedon, Euryades, Leokritos, and many others (21.430). Greatly outnumbered, Odysseus is clearly able to use the help of his newly matured son and the inside information and allies that he brings to cleanse his household of the suitors. There can be no restoration of the household or the polity without purifying them from the evil of the suitors and thereby reestablishing Odysseus as the sole suitor of Penelope and ruler of Ithaka. And there can be no removal of the suitors without Telemachos, so there can be no restoration without the newly matured Telemachos.

7 Yet the mere slaughter of the suitors is not sufficient to accomplish the complete, permanent restoration of household and polity. Perhaps even more important than being able to aid his father in this cleansing, Telemachos's maturity allows him to become a worthy, viable heir of the household and polity. Without such an heir, the long-sought-after restoration of house and kingdom would be temporary at best. If Telemachos were still immature and unfit to rule when Odysseus died (as he eventually must), the great line of Arkeisios, Laertes, and Odysseus would fail. He would be incapable of acting as he should—to boldly give mercy, justice, and protection. The other, inferior Achaians would seize control of Ithaka and Telemachos's household. It is clear, however, that Telemachos, precisely because he has spent most of the time of the epic maturing, is ready to act as he should in order to govern, and to govern well. He calls an assembly (with Athene's help), elicits the favor of foreign kings such as Menelaos (with Peisistratos's help), and then—without help—maintains a degree of order and justice in a chaotic household filled with the most unruly, unjust people imaginable. If Telemachos is able to rule well under such difficult circumstances, if he is able to defend a beggar from hordes of evil men even in the midst of the "tumult" and defend an innocent singer and herald from his father in the midst of his *aristeia* as well as deal out deadly justice to those that deserve it, then he will surely be able deal out justice and mercy in less demanding circumstances (18.399). Thus, there is hope for the future of Ithaka and Odysseus's progeny. Only because Telemachos has accomplished his key action of becoming a mature man is he fit to be heir, and only because he is a worthy heir is the household and polity completely and permanently restored.

8 Telemachos alone is able to successfully aid in the restoration of the household and polity of Odysseus, as he is essential to accomplishing the plot to destroy the suitors and to providing a worthy heir to rule. And he is only able to accomplish these feats because he completes his essential action of maturing from an immature boy to a mature man capable of acting as he ought to. He may not be the *Odyssey*'s protagonist, nor the man for whom the epic is named, but he is essential to the central action of the poem.

Appendix 1

Works Cited

Homer. *The Odyssey of Homer*. Trans. Richard Lattimore. New York: HarperPerennial, 1967.

Appendix 2

Evaluation Standards for Essays

Craft	Quality of Craft	OAChapters. Paragraphs
	A—B—C—D—F	
Invention		
Assignment		2.1
Focus		2.2
Argument/Thesis		2.3
Development/Logic		2.4–14
Evidence		2.15–17
Organization		
Introduction		3.4–7
Body		3.8–10
Conclusion		3.11–13
Paragraphing		3.14
Transitions		3.14
Style		
Diction		4.4–6
Grammar		4.5 and 7–11
Punctuation		4.5 and 7–11
Variation		4.7–15
Mechanics/Citation		Appendix 1

General Comments

Appendix 3

Peer-Review Form

Please read your peer's essay and comment upon the following questions in the margins of the essay, offering revision advice wherever appropriate:

1. Does the essay address the assignment?

2. Is the essay's focus sharp enough, given the assignment's expectations?

3. What is the thesis? Is it determinate and encompassing enough?

4. Are its ideas developed enough? Are its logic and topics strong?

5. Is its textual explication full, and are its analysis and synthesis persuasive?

6. Is the introduction strong: Does it provide an outline of proofs and the thesis?

7. Is the body strong: Do the proofs cohere?

8. Is the conclusion strong?

9. Are the paragraphs unified and coherent?

10.   Are the transitions between parts, paragraphs, and sentences strong?

11.   Is the diction appropriate, precise, concise, and vivid?

12.   Is the grammar correct?

13.   Is the punctuation correct?

14.   Are the periods varied in length and pattern? Are there any strong metaphors?

15.   Is the essay formatted properly?

Works Cited

Aristotle. *Nicomachean Ethics*. Trans. Terence Irwin. Indianapolis: Hackett, 1985.

_____. *Metaphysics*. Trans. W. D. Ross. Oxford: Clarendon Press, 1924.

_____. *Poetics*. Loeb ed. Ed. and trans. Stephen Halliwell. Cambridge, Mass.: Harvard University Press, 1995.

_____. *Rhetoric*. Trans. George A. Kennedy. New York: Oxford University Press, 1991.

Austen, Jane. *Pride and Prejudice*. Oxford: Oxford University Press, 1990.

Berry, Wendell. "Standing by Words." *Standing by Words*. San Francisco: North Point Press, 1983. 24–63.

Booth, Stephen. *An Essay on Shakespeare's Sonnets*. New Haven, Conn.: Yale University Press, 1969.

Corbett, Edward. *Classical Rhetoric for the Modern Student*. 3rd ed. New York: Oxford University Press, 1990.

Darwin, Charles. *The Origin of Species*. Ed. J. W. Burrow. New York: Penguin, 1968.

DiLorenzo, Ray. *Peitho: A Classical Rhetoric*. Manuscript in author's possession.

Elbow, Peter. *Writing with Power: Techniques for Mastering the Writing Process*. New York: Oxford University Press, 1981.

Euclid. *The Thirteen Books of the Elements*. 2nd ed. Trans. with intro. and comm. Sir Thomas L. Heath. New York: Dover, 1956.

Gordon, Karen Elizabeth. *The Deluxe Transitive Vampire: The Ultimate Handbook of Grammar for the Innocent, the Eager, and the Doomed*. New York: Pantheon Books, 1993.

Homer. *Iliad*. Trans. Richard Lattimore. Chicago: University of Chicago Press, 1951.

———. *Odyssey*. Trans. Richard Lattimore. New York: HarperPerennial, 1967.

James, Henry. "The Art of Fiction." *Tales of Henry James*. Ed. Christof Wegelin. New York: Norton, 1984. 345–62.

Johnson, Samuel. "Preface to *A Dictionary of the English Language*." *Samuel Johnson: Rasselas, Poems and Selected Prose*. Ed. Bertrand H. Bronson. New York: Holt, Rinehart and Winston, 1971. 234–60.

———. "Preface to Shakespeare." Ed. Bertrand H. Bronson. New York: Holt, Rinehart and Winston, 1971. 261–307.

Lakoff, George and Mark Johnson. *Metaphors We Live By*. Chicago: University of Chicago Press, 1980.

King Jr., Martin Luther. "Letter from Birmingham Jail." Ed. Edward Corbett. *Classical Rhetoric for the Modern Student*. 3rd ed. New York: Oxford University Press, 1990. 342–56.

Works Cited

Madison, James. *Federalist* 10. *The Federalist Papers*. New York: Penguin, 1987. 122–28.

Marvell, Andrew. "To His Coy Mistress." *The Norton Anthology of English Literature*. 6th ed. Volume 1. Gen. ed. M. H. Abrams. New York: Norton, 1993. 1420–21.

Miles, Robert, Marc Bertonasco, and William Karns. *Prose Style: A Contemporary Guide*. 2nd ed. Englewood Cliffs, N.J.: Prentice Hall, 1991.

Newman, John Henry. *The Idea of a University*. Garden City, N.Y.: Doubleday, 1959.

Plato. *Phaedrus*. Trans. Alexander Nehamas and Paul Woodruff. Indianapolis: Hackett, 1995.

Rodriguez, Richard. *Hunger of Memory: The Education of Richard Rodriguez*. Boston: David R. Godine, 1982.

The Scribner-Bantam English Dictionary. Ed. Edwin Williams. New York: Bantam Books, 1979.

Thoreau, Henry David. *Walden*. New York: Random House, 1950.

Twain, Mark. *The Adventures of Huckleberry Finn*. *The Norton Anthology of American Literature*. 2nd ed. Volume 2. Ed. Nina Baym, *et al*. New York: Norton, 1985. 26–250.

Weaver, Richard. *The Ethics of Rhetoric*. Chicago: Regnery, 1953.

_____. *A Rhetoric and Composition Handbook*. New York: William Morrow, 1974.

Woolf, Virginia. *A Room of One's Own*. San Diego: Harcourt Brace Jovanovich, 1957.